AUTOMOTIVE TUNE-UPS
for BEGINNERS

By the Author of

HOT RODDING for BEGINNERS
MOTORCYCLING for BEGINNERS
MINIBIKES and MINICYCLES for BEGINNERS

AUTOMOTIVE TUNE-UPS
for BEGINNERS

I. G. EDMONDS

MACRAE SMITH COMPANY
Philadelphia

Manufactured in the United States of America

Published simultaneously in Canada
by George J. McLeod, Limited, Toronto.

7404

Library of Congress Cataloging in Publication Data

Edmonds, I   G
   Automotive tune-ups for beginners.

   1. Automobiles—Maintenance and repair. I. Title.
TL152.E34   629.28'8   73–21722
ISBN 0–8255–3020–2

All photographs were taken by the author

CONTENTS

Introduction

Why Bother?

After a new car is broken in and the dealer's checkup brings it up to specs (specification), it will run as well as it is ever going to run as a stock engine.

Unfortunately engines wear as they run. This wear—and possibly tear—upsets the careful adjustments to specs made when the car got its delivery shakedown. As this wear continues, engine performance will be poorer and poorer.

The engine won't start as easily in the morning as it once did. When you do get rolling, it may go by fits and starts—jerking and stalling until it gets warmed up. It won't have the old pep. You tramp down on the gas but the old mill takes its time getting up to speed. And you find yourself laying out a bit more for gas each time you pull into a filling station.

Yet there's nothing basically wrong with a car that starts acting up like this. An engine is something like a marching column of soldiers where every soldier has to be in step or else the soldier behind will step on the heels of the soldier ahead and the march becomes disorganized. As to our sluggish engine, a mechanic would say that it needs a "tune-up," which merely means adjusting the engine's ignition and carburetion systems back to their original factory specs. A straight motor tune-up is not automobile repair. It does not involve heavy work, nor does it require a lot of knowledge of mechanics.

Although tuning a car is not a major job, a service-station tune-up can be expensive. The price depends on whether you need a "minor" or a "major" tune-up, what kind of car you have, and how many accessories it has. What have accessories got to do with it? Well, if you have an air conditioner and a lot of smog devices under the hood, the tune-up specialist *may* have to remove them to get at the spark plugs and the distributor. This takes *time*—and it is the mechanic's time more than the price of parts that can make the bill look like the national debt.

Prices vary with different localities and with the going hourly rate for a mechanic's time. An average tune-up will nick your wallet for a minimum of $24 up to as much as $100. You'll often see tune-ups advertised at startlingly low prices, but if you look closely at the ad you'll see that the fine print under the price says, "plus parts."

Why Not Do Your Own Tune-Ups?

With tune-up prices running so high, many car owners choose to let things ride. The old heap doesn't run as well as it used to, but it still gets you to work!

There's more to it than this. Listen to what the owner of a large towing service said to me not so long ago: "Ninety percent of the calls I get to tow in a stalled car are the result of trouble in the ignition system. In just about every case, the real cause was that the engine was allowed to go too long without a tune-up."

That sums it up pretty well. If you don't keep your car tuned it will gradually run worse until it finally quits on you. The high cost of garage tune-ups is no excuse for letting things go—because you can do it yourself. The job doesn't require a lot of knowledge of mechanics or very many special tools. Anybody who can twist a screwdriver and follow directions can do it.

More Reasons for Tune-ups

We mentioned poor performance and possible road break-downs as major reasons for keeping your engine tuned. There are other reasons. Poor performance in an engine can lead to damage that may require expensive repairs. Poor timing, for example, can burn your valves or even wear holes in your pistons. Prolonged cranking at starting, caused by poor points or plugs, can ruin your battery. And just to mention one more of perhaps a hundred examples, I once knew a driver who had a "flat" spot in his acceleration—when he stepped on the gas there was a momentary hesitation before the engine grabbed and moved out. One day he was caught in a bind on the freeway. There was a pile-up in front of him and he couldn't stop in time. He swerved into a crowded adjoining lane, think-ing he could make it. He might have made it in a well-tuned car, but that is what he wasn't driving. The old bus wheezed when it should have snorted, and an oncoming car plowed into him.

The Smog Problem

In the last few years another important reason has arisen for tuning up a car. This is *smog*. A survey made in 1972 for the Federal Environmental Protection Agency revealed that regu-lar tune-ups would reduce smog from exhaust emission by as much as 50 percent.

Thus tune-ups are rapidly becoming necessary as more and more localities pass smog-control laws. California has some very tough regulations. New Jersey became the first state to pass a law requiring mandatory vehicle-emission tests. Chicago then became the first American city to begin testing vehicle exhausts. New York has a similar law relating to vehicles for hire, although it has not yet been enforced. Arizona and Colorado, among other states, are looking into the automobile smog problem.

All this means that drivers are not going to get away with driving untuned cars much longer. Tune-ups are going to be forced on them as a means of cleaning up the air.

Sure, You Can Do It Yourself!

We have said that you can tune your own car, even if your knowledge of mechanics is limited. You might even do a *better* job than a service station because you can spend more time and care than the mechanic can afford to profitably. In fact, an increasing number of car owners are now doing their own work. In its January 1, 1973, issue *Newsweek* magazine had a long article on what it called "do-it-yourself auto repairs." This pastime seems to be booming almost as much as do-it-yourself home repairs were a few years ago.

When you first mention to a beginner that he can make his own tune-ups, he has a number of questions. Here are some of them, with the answers:

"Is it hard to do?"   No, it isn't. This is because a tune-up does not involve massive teardown, nor does it require a lot of experience in diagnosing motor ills. It consists mainly of adjusting elements in the carburetor and the distributor, and changing the points and the condenser.

"Are all cars tuned the same?"   Well, yes and no. You do just about the same things to all cars, but you do them in a different way. However, they all work on the same principles. If you understand the principles, then it is very simple to figure out what you have to do. For example, the electronic distributors that Chrysler used on its 1973 automobile do not use the points and condensers you find on other cars. Yet the distributor, despite these omissions, has the same job—to send a pulse of high-powered electricity to each spark plug at the right time.

Similarly, the Wankel rotary engine you've been hearing so much about is indeed revolutionary, but its twin distributors are there for the same reason as in a piston engine—to distribute spark to the right plug at the right time.

The big factor in tuning different cars is that you will have to use the appropriate specs, which tell you how much you have to adjust that particular engine. Specs vary greatly not only from make to make but also from model to model. They are provided you by the manufacturer.

"Are some cars easier to tune than others?" A four-cylinder car like a Pinto has only half the cylinders of a V-8 such as a Chevrolet. This makes things a little easier. The main difficulty in any tune-up job is getting to the things you have to adjust. Some designers place the distributor way back under the hood where it is difficult to get at. Then they cram in an air-conditioning unit that makes it hard to reach the sparkplugs. Sometimes these bigger engines are crammed so tight into body wells that you have to use universal joints on your socket wrenches or offset tools to get to your plugs and distributor hold-down bolts. As a general rule, four- and six-cylinder engines have more room under the hood than V-8's and are easier to work with for that reason.

"What about tools? Must I spend more for special tools than I'll ever save doing my own work?" You can divide your tool needs into two lists. One includes those you must have just to get by. The other list includes those you can use to an advantage and which you should get someday.

These tools you must have:
1. Medium bit screwdriver
2. Set of small ignition wrenches
3. Sparkplug wrench
4. Set of open-end wrenches (for loosening the distributor hold-down bolt and for removing fuel lines)
5. Pair of needle-nose pliers

6. Feeler gauge for setting points and plugs
7. Compression gauge
8. Timing light
9. Tach/dwell meter

If you have a Delco-Remy window-set distributor, then you'll need a hex wrench to adjust your points.

None of these tools is very expensive. You should be able to save enough money on your first tune-up to pay for everything you need. After that you are home free. Of course, after you get the bare essentials you can keep adding such valuable things as a belt-tension gauge, engine analyzer, locknut screwdrivers, etc. You might even go so far as to plunk down $2,000 to $4,000 for an electronic scope if you're really interested in going first class. However, you can get by with the above list as a starter.

The most expensive item on our beginner's list is the tach/-dwell meter. Its job is to tell how fast the engine is running (revolutions of the crankshaft per minute), and the length of time the distributor points are closed. The one I use cost me $19.95 at Sears. You can get them for as little as $12.50. The timing light, needed to insure that the spark plugs ignite the gasoline mixture at the precise instant, costs no more than $2.50 or so for the neon type. They work, but the glow is so weak that you can't see it in a bright light. However, it's good enough to learn with.

"I haven't much time. How long does it take to tune a car?" The actual working time should not run more than a half hour to an hour. If your carburetor is gummed up and you have to use a cleaner, you may have to let it soak a half hour or more, depending on manufacturer's recommendations for the particular cleaner.

"Do I have to buy anything besides tools?" What you have to buy in the way of parts, cleaners, and the like depends on what is wrong with your engine. These will represent no extra expense over a service station tune-up, which would

charge you for them anyway. For a home tune-up job you'll need:

- A tune-up kit consisting of a set of points, a condenser, and a new rotor.
- New distributor cap (optional).
- Carburetor overhaul kit (optional).
- New set of spark plug wires (if existing wiring is worn or defective).
- New battery (if present battery checks out bad).
- New PCV valve.

So you see no one can tell you what you are going to need in the way of parts, wires, belts, and valves until you check things out.

How Do You Do It?

If you know a little something about cars, what we've said here so far is probably completely understandable to you. If you are a total beginner, you may be confused by such terms as "carburetor," "distributor," "PCV valve" and so on.

Don't get discouraged. The purpose of this book is to provide a road map for the beginner. We intend to take each successive step in simple engine tune-up procedures and explain what to do. We'll explain at the same time *why* you do it, *what* you do it with, and what each part is.

Though not essential, it would be a big help to you as a beginner to obtain the manufacturer's shop manual for your car. Many public libraries stock these manuals for the more popular cars.

Now if you can get one of these shop manuals, why do you need the book you have in your hands? One look at a shop manual and you'll know the answer. The shop manual is written by the automobile manufacturer for *trained* mechanics. Consequently, it is very good—but it presupposes too much for a *beginner*.

Picking up one such manual, I see that it has six pages on

tune-ups. We have written an entire book on just the "elementary" elements alone. The difference is that in the shop manual the trained mechanic needs to know only the specs for this particular model and any differences between it and the previous model.

Consider the following direct quote from a shop manual:

> *Contact Set Replacement.* The contact point set is replaced as a complete assembly. The service replacement contact set has the breaker lever spring and point alignment preadjusted at the factory. Only the dwell angle (point opening) requires adjustment after replacement. Rough contacts that are "grayish" in color have a greater area of contact than new contacts and will provide satisfactory service until most of the tungsten is worn off. Pitted or transferred contacts is a normal condition and should not necessarily be replaced unless the transfer has exceeded .020 inches."

This is all the manual has to say about replacing points. It's enough for a trained mechanic, who knows what is meant by "preadjusted breaker lever spring" and "transferred contacts." But somebody just starting his first tune-up may be a bit bewildered.

Our purpose in this book is to guide the beginner step-by-step through the basic elements of engine tune-up. At the end you should be able to do a simple tune-up job yourself and have the basic knowledge to go on into advanced tune-up work.

Before we get into the actual work on distributor and carb, we must take a few minutes out to explain how an engine works. We are not going to throw around a lot of technical terms like Ohm's law and residual magnetism, or formulas like $W = F \times D$. such things—especially Ohm's law—are very valuable but confusing to a beginner, and are not really essen-

This photo of a Ford Thunderbird engine shows how the carburetor A, the coil B and the distributor C are mounted in the center of the engine between the two banks of cylinders in a V-8 engine. The battery D is mounted to the side in this particular car. The object marked E is of interest because it is the starter solenoid. Later we will use it to connect it to a remote starter cable.

tial to getting him started. Later, if you go deeper into tune-ups, you can pick up the heavy technical stuff you need to know.

So, to begin, let's see how an engine works.

AUTOMOTIVE TUNE-UPS for BEGINNERS

Chapter 1

FIRE AND GAS

Before you can work on something you should know what you are working on. This may seem self-evident, but you'd be surprised how many people have little or no idea of what goes on under the hood of their cars.

I know a man who argued heatedly with me just recently that the electricity that fires a car's plugs goes through the points to the plugs. As proof he cited the fact that points get burned. He further insisted that he had been changing his own points and timing his own engines for ten years.

As a matter of fact, he did change the points in his car and he did time his engine. He accomplished this by following direction he had been given. But he was absolutely wrong about the path the electrical current takes from battery to sparkplug.

Okay, so he was wrong about a technicality. He still got the job done, didn't he? You can say he *partly* got the job done. He knew that if his car started missing because the points were burned he should change them, but he didn't have enough knowledge about the working of his engine's electrical system to discover why his points burned out so quickly.

1

The major reason for repairing anything is to know how it is supposed to work when it's working right. Then when something goes wrong all you have to do is check over the thing's cycle of operation until you find what isn't putting out as it should.

With this in mind, let's first review very quickly and non-technically how an automobile engine is supposed to work.

This Is an Engine

An internal combustion automobile engine is basically a block of metal with a number of round holes—called *cylinders* —bored in it. Their job is to act as bottles to hold the gas vapor that the engine burns for fuel. Since the holes are bored all the way through this block of metal, the cylinders must have stoppers at each end to keep the gas vapor from escaping.

The top plug is a *cylinder head* which acts as a cap across all the cylinders. It has holes in it for the *intake* and *exhaust* valves. They open and close to let air/gas (fuel) mixture into the cylinder and to let the burned gas out.

The bottom plug for the cylinder is a piston. It fits into each cylinder hole and has rings around it to give it a tight fit so that no fuel will leak out through the bottom. The cylinder head at the top is in one piece and fits across the top of all the cylinders, but each cylinder has its own piston.

This piston moves up and down in the cylinder. The bottom of the piston is hinged to a *connecting rod.* The connecting rod is fastened to a *crankshaft.* All the other pistons in the engine are likewise connected to the crankshaft by their rods.

An air/gas fuel mixture is fed into the cylinders one at a time through the intake valve. When you step on the starter an electric starting motor causes the crankshaft to turn. Turning the crankshaft causes the pistons to rise in the cylinders. As each piston reaches the top of its cylinder, the air/gas mixture in that cylinder is squeezed (compressed) into a small space in the cylinder head. Then an electric spark from a sparkplug set in the cylinder head ignites the compressed fuel mixture. It burns with terrific speed, producing expanding gases that push the piston down with great force.

As the pistons are pushed down by the burning gases, they force the crankshaft to turn or spin. The spinning of the crankshaft causes the drive train to turn, which moves the car's rear wheels.

This shows an engine block with the cylinder head, push rods and all other parts removed to show the cylinder holes with the pistons inserted. The piston at the left is near Top Dead Center (which is as high as it can rise). The piston at the far right is near Bottom Dead Center (as low as it can go). The two pistons in between are in different stages of rising and descending. A four-cylinder engine would have just this number of cylinders and pistons. A six-cylinder engine would have six in a straight line, while an eight-cylinder V-8 engine would have two banks of four cylinders just like this mounted in a V angle to each other so that the connecting rods from each bank could connect with a common crankshaft.

The Fuel System

The foregoing explanation was too simple. There is much more to an automobile engine than all that. However, this book is about tune-ups, not automobile overhaul. Accordingly we will leave out explanations of such things as valve lifters, rocker arms, main bearings, camshafts, timing chains, and many other essential parts. They are not involved in engine tune-up and to bring them in now would only get us off the subject.

In tune-up our major concerns are:

- Getting the right mixture of air and fuel into the cylinder.
- Getting the spark to fire the mixture at just exactly the right split second.

We mentioned earlier that the fuel we burn comes into the cylinder through the intake valve. Here is how the fuel gets to the intake valve in the first place:

- The fuel starts as liquid gasoline in our gas tank.
- A fuel pump in the line pulls the liquid gasoline from the gas tank to the *carburetor,* which sits on top of the engine. The carburetor is nothing but a mixing machine. It sucks air down through its throat and sprays liquid gasoline into the air, thus mixing the air and gas together into a vapor. (This is necessary because liquid gasoline will not burn, but gasoline *vapor* will burn when mixed with the proper amount of air. If there is too much air in the mix, it will be too *lean* to burn. If there is too much gas in the mix, it will be too *rich* to burn. One of the jobs of the carburetor is to get the mixture just right. And one of the jobs of tune-up is to adjust the carburetor so it will make the right mixture.)
- The properly mixed air/gas volume goes from the carburetor to the *intake manifold*. This is a chamber designed to hold the fuel mixture until the proper inlet valve opens to let the fuel flow into the cylinder to be fired.

The Four-Stroke Engine

At this point it is well to understand about an engine's strokes. All automobile engines, except for the rotary Wankel and "midgets" employing motorcycle engines, are *four-stroke engines,* or more correctly, "four-stroke-cycle" engines. This means that each piston must make four movements in the cylinder for each firing of a sparkplug. These four strokes are two movements up and two movements down in the cylinder. Each of the pistons must make these four strokes.

The accompanying diagram shows one cylinder going through its four strokes. In the first diagram the piston is going down on the *intake stroke.* The inlet valve is open and the air/gas mixture is flowing in from the intake manifold. The stroke ends when the piston reaches Bottom Dead Center (BDC) which is as far as it can go.

In the second diagram the piston starts to rise again for the second stroke, or *compression stroke.* The inlet valve has now closed and the rising piston is squeezing (compressing) the gas mixture into a small area in the cylinder head.

This compression stroke is very important in tune-up work, as we will discover shortly.

Just before the piston reaches Top Dead Center—the highest point in its rise—the sparkplug ignites the fuel mixture with a flash of electricity across the electrodes of the plug. This flash of fire must come just at the right time. This stroke ends when the piston reaches Top Dead Center.

The burning gases push the piston down with great force. This is the *power stroke* that spins the crankshaft and makes the car run. It is completed when the piston reaches Bottom Dead Center. This is the third of our four strokes.

The fourth or last of the four-stroke cycle is the *exhaust* stroke. As the piston rises on this final stroke, the exhaust valve

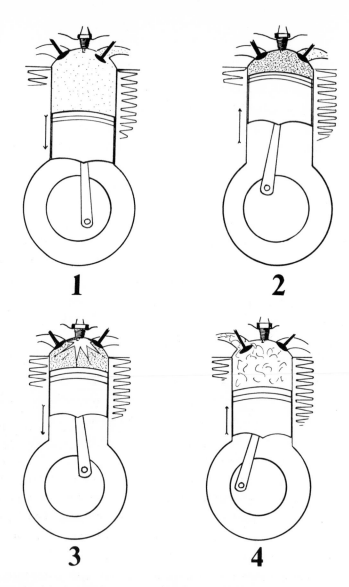

1

2

3

4

Principle of the four-stroke engine. *On stroke one the piston is pulled down by the turning crankshaft. At the same time the intake valve opens and the fuel-air mix from the carburetor is drawn into the cylinder. Stroke two is when the piston goes up again. With both intake and exhaust valves closed, the fuel-air mix is compressed into the small area of the combustion chamber at the top of the cylinder. Stroke three is the power stroke. The burning gas, ignited by the spark plug, forces the piston down, transferring power to the crankshaft. Stroke four is the exhaust stroke. The rising piston pushes the burned gases out through the open exhaust valve.*

opens and the rising of the piston pushes the burned gases from the cylinder.

The exhaust valve closes when the piston reaches TDC. This ends the four-stroke cycle. The piston then starts down on the intake stroke to start a new four-stroke cycle. This goes on as long as the engine is running.

The Ignition System

The next thing to consider is the source of the spark from the sparkplug that ignites the fuel. A car's ignition system begins with the car's battery. When you turn on the ignition, electricity flows from the battery through the ignition switch to the ignition coil.

Since 1956 all new automobiles have been equipped with 12-volt batteries. Voltage in electricity means pressure. So a 12-volt battery does not tell us how strong the battery is, but how much pressure is behind the electricity to move it over the wires.

As we pointed out in telling how an engine runs, the electricity from the battery jumps across the electrodes of the sparkplug to create the spark that fires the fuel. A 12-volt force is not strong enough to jump across this gap in the sparkplug. It has to be built up to as much as 20,000 volts to do the job. This is where the ignition coil comes in. It takes the incoming 12-volt source and steps it up to 20,000 volts. Later, when we go through the routine of tuning up an engine, we'll tell how this is done.

So the battery current goes to the coil for increased voltage or pressure. This high-tension current then passes over the coil wire to the distributor. The distributor does just what its name implies. It distributes the incoming current to each of the spark plugs one at a time *at the correct time,* so that each charge of fuel in the cylinders burns when it should.

You will notice that we have repeatedly said such things as

"at the right time." These things do not always do their thing at the right time, and that is where tuneup comes in.

Summing Up

To sum up what we have said in this chapter, an engine runs because fuel is pumped from the gas tank to the carburetor, where it is mixed with air to make a gaseous vapor that will burn. This fuel vapor passes to the intake manifold. Then when the intake valves open on the intake stroke the fuel is drawn into the cylinder. The rising piston—on the compression stroke —squeezes the mixture into the cylinder head, where a spark- plug ignites it just before the piston reaches Top Dead Center. The electricity that provides the ignition spark comes from the battery and is stepped up in voltage by the coil before it passes to the distributor to be shunted in turn to each of the cylinder sparkplugs.

Since we are working only with the ignition system and the fuel system in tuning a car, it is not necessary to know any more than what has been just covered about the general oper- ation of an automobile engine. Of course, the more you know and understand engines the better off you are. If you intend to go on beyond tune-ups into minor and major repairs, then a fuller knowledge of automobile fundamentals is essential.

But here we are dealing only with an introduction to tuning a car and hence do not need go any deeper into the subject. If you understand generally how the fuel and ignition systems work, you have the foundation upon which we can build step by step the procedures for tuning your car.

Of the things we have discussed to this point, the most important to remember are these terms:

Compression. This means squeezing the air/gas fuel mix- ture in the cylinder as much as the engine design will let us. The more the fuel is compressed, the greater power the burn- ing fuel will exert on the top of the piston to make the car run.

The four major items we are concerned with in engine tune-up are shown in this front view of a small Ford engine. To make the view clear, the engine's radiator has been removed. A is the air cleaner, which sits atop the carburetor. B is the distributor. C is the ignition coil. D is the pointer, which must be lined up with the timing marks on the fan-belt pulley. These same items will be found on all cars, but in different shapes and positions.

Copy

Compression is important to us as tune-up specialists because a car with poor compression cannot be tuned properly. One of the first steps in tune-ups is to check the cylinders' compression. If they test out bad, you're stuck with an overhaul job. Poor compression can be caused by worn piston rings, burned or poorly seated valves, or even a leaking head gasket.

Compression Stroke. The compression stroke is the movement of the piston from its lowest position to its top position while compressing the fuel mixture. If we should accidentally turn our engine while we have the distributor removed to work on it, we must be able to determine the position of the compression stroke in order to replace the distributor properly so that the original firing sequence is maintained.

Top Dead Center. This is the position of the piston in its cylinder when the crankshaft has pushed it as high as it can go. We have a Top Dead Center (TDC) on both the compression stroke and the exhaust strokes, but in tuning we will be using the TDC on the compression stroke to "time" our engine so that the spark occurs just at the right split second.

With this necessary background out of the way, we can now begin to tune up an engine, proceeding step by step.

Chapter 2

GETTING READY TO WORK

You're ready to begin. Where do you start? Most shop manuals say you should check your engine's compression to see if it worth tuning.

That you should do—but quite a bit further down the line. There are several important things you should do first.

Safety is the first thing to consider. A tune-up, since it does not involve pulling engines, lifting heavy parts, turning large bolts, and working under the car, is not as dangerous as automobile repairs. But there are still plenty of ways a careless person can pick up an unwanted quota of cuts, bruises, and bumps—or even lost fingers and broken bones.

It's Always Carelessness or Lack of Knowledge

Carelessness is the cause of most shop accidents. Lack of knowledge generally causes the rest.

Some of the things that can happen are nothing short of fantastic. One homemade mechanic, who obviously needed glasses, had difficulty seeing the timing marks as they were lighted by his strobe. He stuck his head down closer and closer until the spinning fan sliced into the tip of his nose.

In a similar accident, a tuner's foot slipped as he leaned over to point a timing light at the marks on the pulley. His hand hit the spinning fan. Now he has only nine fingers.

Sometimes an unsafe act can start a chain reaction. This Rube Goldberg mess actually happened: A beginner reached down to brace himself as he bent over to take a closer look at his carburetor. He wasn't watching. He put his hand squarely on the hot manifold. This made him jerk back. He bumped against an open can of oil on the work bench behind him. The oil spilled on the floor, but he was too interested in getting in the house and putting something on his burned hand to pay attention to the oil spill. When he came out again he slipped on the oil and cracked his wrist in the fall.

There is, of course, a bright side to his troubles. He got a thorough lesson in shop safety.

Know What You're Doing

If you aren't familiar with a job, read and follow directions carefully. It is impossible for any set of directions to be complete enough to cover every contingency, so you have to use a little thought in your work.

Consider one sad example. A beginner was following a checklist of things to do in tuning a car. He got along fine until he came to the part that said to check the fan belt for tension. There is a test gadget made to do this, but if you don't have one, then you stick your finger under the belt and lift it. The belt should give about half an inch and no more. If it is looser than that, then you tighten the belt.

That sounded simple enough. So he stuck his finger under the belt to lift up. His only mistake was that the engine was running. His finger was mashed between the belt and the generator pulley. Maybe this sounds stupid, but mistakes like this are easy to make when one is just learning and becomes interested in what one is doing.

Rules for Safety

Most rules for safety in the home garage are just plain common sense. Here are a few of those most frequently violated, resulting in accident or injury.

- Don't wear loose clothing, rings, or wrist watches when you work. They are easy to catch on something.
- Keep the floor clean. Slips and stumbles will be your reward if you don't.
- Don't crawl under a car that is supported only by a jack. Use wheel stands.
- If you use rags to wipe your engine, place them in closed metal containers. Spontaneous combustion can burn down your garage *and* your house.
- Do not run the engine in a closed garage. Carbon monoxide is more deadly than a rattlesnake, because it doesn't rattle to warn you.
- Always disconnect the battery cable when you work on the fan, starter, or anything else that might start accidentally.
- Keep your tools free from grease and make sure they fit the bolt you're working on. A slipped wrench means a cracked knuckle unless you're very lucky.
- Never smoke around a battery. The storage batteries used in cars give off hydrogen gas. It is extremely explosive.

Clean It Up

Probably the best way to start a tune-up is to clean your engine. A few genuine car lovers will keep their mills shining, but the majority of us just let things go until the engine is caked with grease and dirt. This not only leads to possible electrical shorts but can hide a lot of potential trouble. The first thing you need to do is to inspect the engine and wiring for breaks, cracks, and shorts. You can't do this if the engine is hidden under oily grime.

Cleaning an engine is simple enough. There are a number of prepared cleaners containing grease solvents. You run the engine until it is warm, spray on the solvent, let it stand according to the directions, and then hose off the goo with a spray of water.

The only precaution is to cover the distributor with some plastic sheeting or other waterproof material to keep it from getting wet and possibly shorting out when you try to start the engine. Also cover the alternator to keep water out of it.

Checking the Wiring

The ignition system begins with the battery. That is where you start checking out the wiring. You can start your routine something like this:

- Check the battery cables. There are two. One leads to the starter; the other is connected to the frame of the car. Check the cables for tight fit on the battery terminals. Are they worn or frayed? Are the connections tight where the ground wire attaches to the car frame? I once had a car refuse to start because rust had gotten in between the ground wire and the frame. This broke the electrical circuit. A wire brush to brighten up the metal where ground wire and frame are connected fixed the trouble.
- Check the wires leading to and from the coil. There are three of them. Are the connections tight? Is the wire insulation cracked? Are the wires dirty, oil-soaked, or kinked?
- Now check the wires coming from the coil to the distributor. There'll be two. One is a heavy wire running from the center of the coil to the center of the distributor. This is the high-tension wire. The second wire runs from a terminal on the side of the coil to the side of the distributor. This is the primary wire. As before, look for poor connections and poor wiring.

• Next inspect the wires running from the distributor to the sparkplugs. These are heavy wires since they carry high-tension current. They look substantial but are actually rather delicate. Originally all sparkplug wires had copper wire cores, which were less likely to give trouble, but in the last few years more and more cars use the TVRS type of resistance wire. Ordinary copper wires send out signals that are picked up on radios and TVs as static. In the place of the copper wire to carry the current, TVRS wires use carbon, which acts to suppress static or interference. The carbon is impregnated in linen, nylon, or glass fiber threads to give it strength. Because such wires are much more easily broken than copper, great care must be taken to avoid bending or kinking them and in pulling them off the sparkplugs and out of the distributor towers.

The Correct Way to Pull

The correct way to remove a high-tension wire is to grasp the wire by the boot. The boot is the rubber or plastic covering at the end which fits down over the plug or tower to give a tight, waterproof fit.

The boot fits tight, and heat and grime usually cause it to stick. Never grab the wire and pull up. Grasp the boot in your fingers and turn it, first to the right and then to the left until you break the seal. Then, still holding the boot, pull up slowly.

If the boots are broken or chewed up at the ends, they should be replaced.

The plastic sheathing used on some of these wire go bad very easily. Oil and grease cause them to crumble. So, in this first eyeball check, we inspect every one very carefully.

Something's Missing

The importance of good wiring cannot be overemphasized. Bad wiring can add resistance. Resistance is anything that makes it harder for electricity to flow through the wires. It can be caused by poor connections, by corroded connections where the rust or corrosion acts like a dam to hold back part or all of the electricity, or by small breaks. All of these lower the voltage, giving a poorer spark at the plug. Or the resistance may be so bad that the plug will fail to fire at all. "Missing," a mechanic would say.

Many times a car owner will blame his battery when his trouble is really poor wiring. Later we will go into how to test our wires. Right now we are concerned only with "eyeballing" it—making a visual check for obvious troubles before we get down to serious testing.

Some cars have clips mounted on the engine to hold the sparkplug wires from bouncing around. This is good, but in time the natural vibration of the engine can create enough friction between the wire holders and the wire insulation to wear through the insulation.

You won't notice this happening much on low-mileage cars, but when the old heap starts getting up in years this is something to watch out for.

I knew one driver who complained that he couldn't start his car in the mornings, but if he came back in the afternoon the contrary thing kicked off with no trouble. The first thing a mechanic would consider in a case like this is choke trouble. All cars need to be choked when they are cold—which means reducing or "choking" the amount of air going into the carburetor so that the gas/air mix will be richer.

The choke checked out okay. So did the heat riser, which is a flapper valve on the manifold to throw hot air up through two holes to warm up the carburetor more quickly.

An electrical check showed that battery juice was getting to the coil but not to the plugs. Tracing down the high-tension sparkplug wires from the plugs to the distributor showed that the clip holder had worn holes in the underside of the wires. Because the exposed wires did not rest directly on the metal

To protect wires the boot should be turned back and forth to break the seal before the wire is pulled. This picture shows the boots on the distributor towers. Tower boots are also called nipples.

Here a mechanic checks his sparkplug wires for cracks in the insulation. All tune-ups should begin with an "eyeball" check like this.

holders they did not short out except in the morning when moisture condensed under the wires. This was sufficient to complete the electrical circuit, causing a short that kept the plugs from firing. Once the temperature warmed up, the moisture causing the short dried and the car started easily.

This is a freak situation, but it has happened and it can happen again. It illustrates the things you have to look for when you eyeball your engine. You are searching for any kind of wear, cracks, poor connections, or loose fits that offer resistance to the smooth flow of electricity to the sparkplugs.

While checking your wiring, don't forget to look carefully at the plastic distributor cap. Cracks here can also cause short circuits.

Other Things to "Eyeball"

Your visual check should continue over the engine. Look for oil leaks and gasoline leaks around the carburetor, fuel pump, and fuel lines.

Note particularly the condition of the numerous rubber hoses that snake over and around your engine. If they are cracked, aged, or ill-fitting they can cause nearly as much trouble as poor wires. Some of these hoses are vacuum lines that do a very important job in keeping an engine running right. A leak in a vacuum line may often be the major or only cause of poor engine performance.

Engine vacuum, as we will learn later in discussing individual parts of our engine, has a number of functions in an internal combustion engine. You'll find vacuum doing everything from pulling fuel into the cylinders to running some models of windshield wipers and even advancing timing in the distributor.

The eyeball check should also include the radiator hoses. Here you look for cracks and for "rigidity"—that is, you feel the hose to see if the rubber is still stiff. Often a hose can look good on the outside yet be deteriorating inside. One day the normal vibration of the engine can produced a sudden crack and all your coolant runs out on the road.

The result can be an overheated engine at the best or, at the worst, the pistons may expand and freeze in the cylinders. Also, if the inside of your hoses are going bad, bits of rubber or fabric may get down into the radiator core and block off some of the small passages, again leading to overheating.

Fan-Belt Tension

Finally, you check the tension of the fan belt or belts which operate off a pulley run by the front end of the crankshaft. These belts, if there are more than one, run the fan to cool the radiator, the alternator or generator which recharges the car's battery, smog-system pumps in some cases, and air-conditioning units when the cars are so equipped.

If the fan belt is too loose, it will not properly drive the fan and generator. When you have a battery that will not hold its charge, the trouble is sometimes due to a loose fan belt rather than a failing battery. The same thing is true when an engine overheats. In either case you should always check out your fan belt before wasting time on diagnosing other troubles.

Proper fan-belt tension is checked with a fan-belt tension gauge. They cost about $20. This is pretty steep for shade-tree garage work where you'll only need the special tool a couple of times a year. So, check it this way: *with the engine dead* insert your fingers under the belt between the fan pulley and the generator pulley. Pull up. There should be about ½ inch of give.

If there is more slack than this, you probably aren't getting full service from your generator, air conditioner, fan or any other accessory run off the belt.

If the belt tension is tighter than this, then you are putting undue strain on your pulley shafts and bearings and on the fan belt itself. You'll be wearing both out faster than necessary.

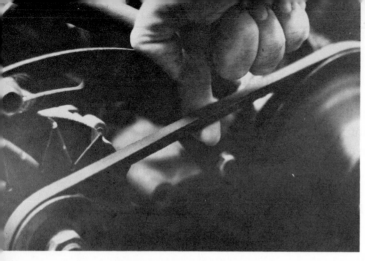

Test fan-belt tension by lifting up on the belt. "Give" should not be more than one half inch. A belt-tension gauge, if you prefer it to the finger-lift method, costs almost $20.

The fan belt is tightened by loosening the bolt indicated by the white arrow and pushing outward on the alternator. The bolt is then retightened. On some models of cars the adjusting bracket is at the top rather than at the bottom of the alternator as shown here.

How to Adjust the Fan Belt

Fan-belt tension is adjusted by loosening a nut holding the generator or alternator. The mounting bracket has an adjustment slot in it. Once the nut is loosened, the generator can be moved toward the engine to loosen the belt or outward from the engine to tighten it. Once the proper position is determined, the adjusting nut is tightened.

It is doubtful if you can pull the generator out enough by hand to get the proper tightening tension. If you can't, then you use a long wrench or piece of pipe as a pry pole. Put it between the generator case and the engine block and pull down until the generator (or alternator) is pushed out enough to get the tension you want on the fan felt.

Before making the adjustment, you should of course inspect the belt for signs of wear. Fan belts don't cost much and a broken one can lead to trouble. Drivers on the desert or remote area are well advised to keep an extra fan belt in their trunks.

Summing It Up

Tune-up begins with proper preparation. We start with:
- A place to work that has good ventilation to prevent carbon monoxide build-up from the running engine.
- A safety check and careful observation of safety rules.
- Proper tools that are clean and not worn; a slipped tool can mean a skinned knuckle or a broken hand.

Then the actual work begins with an "eyeball" check of engine. We look for:
1. Gasoline and oil leaks.
2. Wear on all wires, hoses and belts. These include the battery cable, the battery hold-down strap, the battery ground wire, the coil wires, sparkplug wires, vacuum

hoses, radiator hoses (at top and bottom of radiator), and fan belts.

There is one other important hose that needs to be checked. This is the PCV valve, or Positive Crankcase Ventilation valve. Since it is concerned with the smog-control system, we will come back to it later when we go fully into emission control and smog devices.

We are now ready to go back to the battery and begin work on the entire ignition system.

Chapter 3

THE BATTERY

An automobile's ignition system begins with the battery. The battery is correctly called a "storage battery," although it does not store electricity. Instead it stores "chemical energy" which can be *changed* into electricity. Here's how it works.

A battery is made up of *cells.* Each cell has two plates in it, one positive and the other negative. These plates are covered with a liquid called *electrolyte.* Electrolyte is nothing but 38 percent sulfuric acid (by weight) and the rest pure water. When a path is provided for electricity to flow, the action of the electrolyte on the battery plates breaks down the sulfuric acid, causing the acid's chemical energy to change to electrical energy. This makes electricity flow in the circuit wires.

How much electricity is generated in this way depends upon how many square inches of surface each cell plate has. Thickness of the cell plates has nothing to do with how much electricity is generated. However, thicker plates will make the battery last longer.

The *amount* of electricity a battery puts out is measured in *amperes. The ampere-hours* rating of a battery tells how much juice it will put out.

Since 1956 all car batteries have been 12-volt batteries. You will remember we mentioned earlier that a battery's *voltage* is the pressure behind the juice. It is the strength that moves the amperes along the wires.

We have just said that the ampere rating of a battery depends upon the surface size of the plates in the cell. The more surface exposed to the electrolyte, the more juice you get from the battery and the longer you can grind the starter without running the battery down. However, the plate size affects only the amperage. It has nothing to do with voltage. Each cell produces two volts of pressure, regardless of the battery size.

So, since each cell only kicks out two volts, we must have six cells in every battery in order to get the necessary 12 volts. The six-volt batteries used on pre-1956 cars needed only three cells to get their six-volt charge.

Discharge, Charge, and Discharge

Turning on the ignition switch gives the battery current a path to travel. As the current flows out of the battery the action of the electrolyte on the lead plates causes the lead peroxide on the negative plates to change into lead sulfate. At the same time water is created which dilutes the electrolyte.

This leads to what we call a "discharged battery." Remember, we get our electricity from the action of the electrolyte on the plates. The formation of the lead sulfate and the gradual weakening of the electrolyte as water is created in the battery means that there is less and less electricity created as the sulfate builds up.

This is known to battery men as "sulfation." Sulfation is created naturally as electricity flows *from* the battery. It can also be caused by letting the battery sit unused for too long or by letting the electrolyte get so low in the battery that the plates are exposed to the air.

This natural sulfation could quickly discharge and ruin a battery except for one remarkable thing. Sulfation occurs when electricity flows *out* of the battery, but the whole process is reversed if electricity flows *into* the battery.

So when the battery's charge drops to a certain point we use a generator, operated by the car's engine, to deliver current into the battery. This current changes the lead sulfate back into lead peroxide. In the process the sulfate (SO_2) and water (H_2O) are recombined into sulfuric acid (H_2SO_4) which is electrolyte. The battery is now back in its original "charged" condition and ready to go again.

This process continues as long as the battery is in working condition. If this explanation is confusing, it is not necessary to remember it. It is given here solely to explain why you need a generator to keep your battery charged and why it is important that the liquid level of your battery be kept above the plates by adding pure water when needed. Sulfuric acid does not evaporate, so you never add acid—only water. Distilled water is best because it has all possibly harmful chemicals removed. However, most battery authorities agree that if water is pure enough to drink, it is good enough to use in your battery.

Checking the Battery

If the battery wasn't cleaned when the car was prechecked, this should be done now before going any further. Battery terminals will corrode with acid due to exposure to air. If not removed, this acid will eventually eat through the cable connections and into the cables themselves. Also, acid getting between the terminal and the connector can add a resistance that can drastically cut power.

You begin by checking the battery for cracks, bulges, or warpages. The electrolyte in a discharged battery can freeze in cold weather and crack the case. When it thaws you lose electrolyte and the plates are exposed to sulfation or oxidation from the air. There's nothing you can do here except replace the battery before it goes completely dead on you in the middle of a busy freeway.

The battery case is rectangular or square. Occasionally you will notice that the case looks warped or is bulging on the sides. You can lay a straightedge along the sides of the case to check this. If you find that it is bulging, you may as well head for the auto parts house to order a new battery.

Such bulges are generally due to pressures caused by excessive sulfation, in turn the result of poor recharging or leaving a battery sit for a long time in a discharged condition.

Now we said that running direct current into a battery—via a portable recharger or the engine's generator—will restore the sulfation to its original lead peroxide and sulfuric acid, putting the battery back in operating condition. This is true in ordinary circumstances, *but if the sulfation deposits are too thick or the crystals formed are too large,* the charging current can't get through the heavy barrier (resistance) far enough to turn all the sulfation back. Thus the electrolyte in the battery can't act on the lead plates to generate the juice we need. Your battery is ruined. All you can do is buy another one.

Cleaning the Battery

A dirty battery can discharge itself. So the first thing we do, if it wasn't done in our precheck, is to clean the top of the battery.

If the terminals are corroded with "battery acid," clean them with baking soda. Remember that this acid is not the same acid as the electrolyte and forms as a heavy paste on the outside of the connectors at the terminals. It is caused by the action of the air on the terminals and is highly corrosive. It can eat through your clothes, cause painful burns on your hands, and mess up the car's paint if it gets on the finish. So handle it with care.

Make a thick paste of common household baking soda and

It is best to remove the battery from the car to check it out for anything more than just replacing battery water. Most mechanics put the battery on a work bench, but the floor is O.K. too.

water. Brush this mixture on the terminals and connectors with a small paint brush. The wet soda will fizz as it comes in contact with the acid. After the fizzing stops, wash the combined soda and acid away with a weak stream of water from a hose. If no hose is available, pour water over the terminal with a cup.

If all the acid hasn't been removed, paint on more soda paste and wash off again. Be careful to get to the underside of the terminal as well as the top.

Wipe off the top of the battery and dry it. Be sure the caps are tight so that none of the acid and wash water gets into the battery itself.

When you wash away the acid from the top of the battery, it will run down the sides of the battery and get into the battery frame. It is well to remove the battery and clean the frame too.

Removing the Battery Cables

Few people remove their batteries to clean them, but it is a good idea. The connectors on the cables are difficult to remove from the battery terminal posts. After the adjusting bolt is loosened, it is best to use a special puller made for this purpose. Its two arms hook under the connector. Then a central pusher rod is screwed down. This presses against the terminal post and pulls the connector up. (See illustration.)

Many beginners and some thoughtless old timers pry the connector loose with a heavy screwdriver inserted under the edges. This puts uneven pressure on the sides of the terminal post and may cause internal damage. The puller exerts its pressure straight down on the terminal post and thus eliminates this danger.

However, you can pry the connector loose if you work slowly and carefully. So the puller is a great convenience but not an absolute necessity. They don't cost much, about $2, and are well worth their price. If you do much battery work, the time saved in using them is worth many times the price.

Once the cables are removed, the battery is lifted out of the car and placed on a work bench or on the concrete floor. Batteries are made of lead and are heavy. Care must be taken in removing them, both to avoid dropping and damaging the case and to prevent back strain from lifting so heavy a weight from a stooped position. Special strap carriers are made that slip over the terminal posts.

A cable puller is an easy way to remove battery cables without harming the battery terminal. This tool is a great convenience but not a necessity.

Cleaning the Terminal Posts

If the battery is going to be removed from the car, then it is best to wait until it is out of the car to clean the acid away with soda and water. Take care that none of the battery acid gets on your hands when you take the battery out.

This terminal-post cleaner has a circular wire brush inside that fits over the post. The cap at the top unscrews to uncover a round wire brush for use in cleaning the inside of the connector terminals on the battery cable.

This better grade of hydrometer has a built-in thermometer (arrow). The thermometer helps in adjusting the hydrometer reading when the temperature is above or below 80° F.

After the cables have been removed from the posts and all acid removed with soda, the posts and inside of the cable connectors should be cleaned. The lead oxide that forms on them acts as a resistance to cut down your current.

The best way to clean them is with a special cleaning tool. This is a metal shell with a circular wire brush in it that can fit over the terminal post on the battery. In the opposite end of the cleaner, under a metal cap, is another brush that can be used to clean inside the connectors. You just insert, twist until the metal is bright, wipe clean, and it's done.

If you haven't got such a brush, then some backyard mechanics scrape off the oxide with the blade of a penknife. Scrape evenly and don't gouge the metal so that you can't make good contact when you put the cables back on the terminals.

Protection From Acid Build-up

The acid that forms on the battery terminals is caused by the action of the air. After the terminals have been cleaned and the cables reconnected, a coating on the terminals will protect them from the air and will prevent acid reforming as long as the coating lasts.

At one time petroleum jelly was the standard coating used by battery men. The trouble with petroleum jelly is that it melts under the high temperatures we find in an engine compartment. The grease flows down on top of the battery where it collects dust. Also the heat thins it out and the protection is lost after several weeks.

You can still use it if your budget is tight, but the best terminal protector is a can of a special preparation you can buy in any auto parts store. It comes in an aerosol can. To use, you point it at the terminal and spray on a thin coat. Caution: be sure you get the underneath side as well as the top.

Checking the Charge

There are a number of way of checking the charge in a battery. The most practical for the home mechanic is to use a hydrometer to check the *specific gravity* of the electrolyte.

Specific gravity (sometimes abbreviated to *gravity* by mechanics) tells how much heavier a solution is than plain water.
The specific gravity is measured by a hydrometer, which looks
and acts much like a giant eyedropper. It is nothing more than
a large glass tube with a float inside. A rubber bulb is attached
to the top and there is a small tube at the bottom to insert in
the vents in each battery cell.

To use the hydrometer, unscrew the battery cell caps. Insert
the end of the hydrometer in each well in turn, squeeze the
rubber bulb to drive air out of the glass tube, and release the
bulb so that electrolyte is sucked into the glass tube. This will
cause the float inside the tube to rise with the liquid.

This float is marked with graduation marks showing specific
gravity. You hold up the hydrometer and read the figure on the
float that corresponds to the top level of the liquid in the tube.
This gives you the specific gravity of your electrolyte, *provided*
that the temperature of the electrolyte is 80 degrees Fahren-
heit. If it isn't, the reading gives you a basis to start figuring
from.

But before going into the adding and subtracting necessary
to get a correct specific gravity figure, let's talk a bit more
about what specific gravity really means.

Specific Gravity

Everything has weight, and water is no exception. For the
purpose of measuring different solutions, water has been as-
signed a specific gravity of 1 (one). Since sulfuric acid—which
with water makes up our battery electrolyte—is heavier than
water, the electrolyte will have a higher specific gravity than
that of water.

When the battery is fully charged the specific gravity of the
electrolyte will be about 1.280 times as heavy as plain water.
This means that there is the right amount of sulfuric acid mixed
with the battery water to make the battery put out the needed

amount of electricity for our ignition system.

But you will recall that as electricity flows from the battery, water is formed from the sulfuric acid. This dilutes the sulfuric acid in the solution that remains and the specific gravity of the electrolyte drops.

Therefore the specific gravity of the electrolyte can tell us how much the battery is discharged.

If a battery is fully charged at 1.280 specific gravity at 80° then it will be 75 percent charged at 1.250, and 50 percent charged at 1.220. At 1.130 the charge will be so far gone that the battery is useless.

Charging the battery by sending a current of direct current into it will restore the strength of the sulfuric acid from a low specific gravity to the fully charged 1.280—provided, of course, that the battery is not damaged so badly that it will not hold a charge.

Correcting for Temperature

A hydrometer will give a correct reading only if the temperature of the electrolyte is at 80°F. The reason is that the acid expands with heat and contracts with cold.

Therefore, if the temperature of the electrolyte is 120°F it has expanded with heat. Then when we pull this expanded liquid into our hydrometer there will be less acid in the expanded liquid than in the liquid when it was at a temperature of 80° F.

By the same reasoning, if the temperature is 50°, the electrolyte contracts and there is more acid in any amount we pull out of it in our hydrometer.

If this seems confusing, we might compare the electrolyte to noodle soup. If we stir up a half pot of soup and pour out a bowlful, there will be just so many noodles in with the water. But if we expand the pot of soup by adding water to the top, stir it up, and then pour out a bowlful, we will have less noodles in the bowlful than when we filled the bowl before expanding the soup with water.

On the other hand, if we take the original half-filled pot and boil out half the water, a bowl of soup poured from the pot will have many more noodles per bowl.

Therefore, only when the electrolyte temperature is 80°F will we have a true reading on the hydrometer. For any temperature below or above 80° we must do a little figuring. You add .004 to the reading for each 10° above 80, and subtract .004 for each 10° of temperature below 80.

This does not mean that you have to get involved in higher mathematics in order to find out if your battery is half run down. Here is an example to show how easy it is to figure.

Hydrometer reads   1.250
Electrolyte temperature is   90°F

The rule is to *add* .004 to the hydrometer reading for each 10 degrees of temperature *over* 80°. Thus we obtain

1.250   hydrometer reading
** .004   for the 10 degrees over 80**
1.254   the correct specific gravity

Another example:

Hydrometer reads   1.250
Electrolyte temperature is   50°F

The rule is to subtract .004 for each 10 degrees below 80. So

1.250   Hydrometer reading
** .012   for .004 for each of the 10 degrees below 80,**
**   and at 50° we are 30 below 80**
1.238   the correct specific gravity

Although the hydrometer read 1.250 in both cases, the first example showed a battery slightly more than 75 percent fully charged. The second example showed a battery about 60 percent charged. The difference was caused solely by the temperature.

Determining Temperature

How do you tell the temperature of the electrolyte? You don't look at the thermometer on the garage wall, unless the car has been sitting in the garage for some time and is the same temperature as the surrounding air.

A car that has been sitting out in the sun may have an under-the-hood temperature considerably higher than the surrounding air. A car that has just been run hard may have a pretty high temperature.

Some of the better hydrometers have built-in thermometers that do the work for you. They also have a scale to make figuring the temperature differences easy. The cheaper hydrometers do not. Some of them don't even have gradations and specific gravity scales. They have colored areas reading "good," "partly charged," and "bad." Such hydrometers give only approximate readings. Since you don't have the specific gravity figures, there is no way you can accurately adjust for temperature differences. To get a correct reading with one of them, you have to wait until you get a day with 80-degree temperature.

One way to determine battery temperature, or rather temperature of the electrolyte, is to use one of the glass thermometers made for photographers. It should be all glass and not one of those with a metal frame. The sulfuric acid will attack the metal and probably contaminate the electrolyte.

You're better off to get the right kind of a hydrometer in the first place. A number of special battery testers are on the market. They are all good, but cost a mint. Unless you are doing a lot of battery testing, they cost more than the good you'll get from them.

Battery Tools

You can get by with a small wrench to loosen the terminal bolt and a box of soda to clean off the corrosion. However, there are a lot of tools that make the job easier and better. You can add them to your tool list when you can. They are all worth having.

Terminal puller—to remove terminal connectors from posts ($2).

Hex nut pliers—to loosen terminal bolts ($2.50).

Terminal post spreader—This looks like a pair of crooked nose pliers, but is used to spread the terminal connectors on cables so they can slip easily over the battery posts. If you try to hammer the things on (as so many do) you risk knocking something loose inside ($2.98).

Terminal and post cleaner brush—to remove oxide ($2).

Battery lifter and carrier—to remove the battery from the car with a minimum of strain, danger of dropping, etc. ($6).

Hydrometer—to check specific gravity to determine charge-discharge condition of the battery ($2 and up).

Battery cell tester— for testing batteries ($10).

Battery chargers—to recharge discharged batteries (from about $9 to $40 for chargers suitable for home use).

The average prices given were taken from a well-known auto parts company's 1973 catalog and are used to give a general idea of what you'll have to pay. You may be able to beat the prices a few cents by shopping around. Inflation will probably raise them a bit each passing year.

Charging the Battery

If the battery does not test out at least 75 percent of its full charge, you should bring it up to full charge before going on with the tune-up. As the tune-up proceeds, you'll find yourself using the starter quite a bit. Beginners often have trouble "bumping" the starter to move the engine a very small amount in order to get the distributor cam lined up or the timing marks on the Top Dead Center line. As a result they often run the battery down before they realize it.

Home battery chargers are available and some of them are quite reasonable in price. The cheaper ones don't put out as much current and take longer to bring a battery up to full charge. Prices run from less than $10 for small 2-amp chargers to more than a hundred dollars for a fancy professional job that rolls around on wheels.

One of the handiest kind you can own—if you can afford the price—is a dual-purpose starter booster and charger. On these jobs you flip a switch one way and you have a battery charger, but if your battery is so dead it won't turn over the engine, you flip the switch the other way and it kicks out a current that lets you start most engines with dead batteries in about one minute. Now in the booster setting you are drawing house current through rectifiers that turn it into direct current. You are not charging your dead battery that fast. You are just getting the car started.

Safety First

It is extremely important that you carefully follow the directions that come with your battery charger. I've seen students blow the caps off batteries because they forgot to remove them before hooking up the charger.

A battery gives off hydrogen gas, which is highly explosive. So don't smoke, light open flames, or make any sparks around it. Be sure to cut off the charger before disconnecting the lead wires from the charger to your battery to prevent the possibility of an explosion. Provide plenty of ventilation while the charger is running, and disconnect the cables if you are charging the battery in a vehicle equipped with an alternator.

Summing It Up

- Clean your battery and remove corrosive acid from the posts and terminal connectors with soda water.
- Check the battery for warpage, cracks in the case, worn or frayed cables, loose hold-down mounts, and tight connections.
- Check the battery charge with a battery tester or hydrometer. If you use a hydrometer, remember to adjust for temperature by adding .004 for each 10 degrees above 80°F., and subtracting .004 for each 10 degrees below 80°F.
- If the battery tests out low, have it charged at your local service station or charge it yourself with one of the home chargers available.
- Observe proper safety rules, remembering that a battery produces hydrogen gas, which is extremely explosive.
- Recharge if the temperature-corrected specific gravity is below 1.225.

Chapter 4

COMPRESSION AND THE COIL

Before tracing the course of the electrical current from the battery to the coil and the distributor, where one of the most important jobs of engine tune-up is performed, we should first check the engine compression.

This is important because if an engine's compression is bad you cannot do a satisfactory tune-up job.

Just to recall what compression is, let's go back a bit to our previous discussion about the four-stroke engine. The first stroke is the intake stroke. The piston goes down and sucks the air/fuel mixture into the cylinder. Then the piston rises on the compression stroke. This stroke compresses or squeezes the air/fuel mixture into the small space in the cylinder head when the piston rises to top dead center.

Now the more you squeeze the fuel mix, the more bang it will have when it is ignited by the spark plug. This means more power. This is exactly why we have "high-compression" engines today. A high-compression engine is one that squeezes the fuel in the cylinder into a smaller area than in previous engines. How much it squeezes the fuel is called the "compression ratio." For example, if the cylinder is nine times as large as the area in the cylinder head, then we say the cylinder has a 9:1 compression ratio. If the area in the cylinder head (called the "combustion chamber") is only 1 / 12 the size of the cylinder, then we have a 12:1 compression ratio.

The thing to remember here is that the greater the compression ratio, the more power we get for a given charge of fuel.

When the Compression Is Bad

One of the basic steps in tuning a car is to check the compression. Most tune-up specialists do this directly after servicing the battery.

Each piston is fitted with a compression ring set in a groove around the piston. This ring is intended to give a gas-tight fit between the piston and the cylinder wall so that no gas will leak past when the piston is on the compression stroke.

If the rings in the engine are worn, or the cylinder walls badly scratched, gas will leak under compression and it will be impossible for the cylinder to produce the compression ratio the engine was designed to develop.

A blown head gasket between the block and the cylinder head will also cause a compression leak. Badly burned or ill-fitting valves are another cause of poor compression.

Under these conditions an engine will fail to put out full power. It will run badly. You might even have trouble getting up steep hills if the condition is really bad. You'll burn more gas because so much of it is escaping unburned.

When a car gets in this condition no amount of tuning will make it run right. There is nothing to do but repair the trouble. Such repair jobs go beyond the scope of tune-ups. So we will just mention in passing what has to be done. All these jobs are major repairs, involving tearing down the engine.

If the rings are bad, they must be replaced. This is done by removing the head and the oil pan. The connecting rods must be disconnected from the crankshaft and the piston removed from the cylinder to put in new rings.

If the cylinder is scored or has been rubbed out of round by piston "slap" (uneven movement of a loose piston), you must rebore the cylinder hole and put in an oversize piston to fit the larger bore. This is definitely a major mechanical job.

If the trouble is a blown gasket, the job is easier, but still a problem because you'll have to remove the head, which means disconnecting the valves, valve lifters, and manifolds.

If you need a valve job, you'll still have an upper engine disassembly. The valves will have to be replaced or reground to fit.

We Say, Tune Anyway!

An honest mechanic will give your engine a compression check when you go in for a commercial tune-up. If it checks out bad, he'll tell you that a tune-up is a waste of money because your car will not run any better after it is done. He'll advise you to get your engine overhauled before things get worse.

He's giving you good advice. You're car won't run any better after the tune-up. An engine with ring, gasket, or valve trouble should be repaired.

However, if you are not going to get the repair work done and intend to keep driving the car in spite of its condition, you had best go ahead with a tune-up anyway, even if the car won't run better. Here's why.

Many years ago, before I learned to do my own work, I took the vintage crate I was driving into a service station. I asked for a tune-up. The mechanic pulled a fast compression check and gave me the bad news. I needed a valve job. He explained that nothing he could do to the ignition and carburetor would make the heap run better until I had a major repair job done.

I was then a teenager whose financial position was two knotches below an ordinary pauper. I couldn't afford a major overhaul right then. And after all, the heap was still running. Maybe next month or year.

Two days later she conked out on me in the middle of a highway twenty miles from home. I had to get pulled in at a price that mortgaged my soul for the next six months. The trouble was a faulty condenser in the distributor that grounded the primary circuit so that I couldn't get fire to the spark plugs.

Checking and replacing a condenser is one of the basic elements of a tune-up. So, even if my faulty valves, poor rings, and worn camshaft would have kept a tune-up from making my wreck run better, a tune-up would have saved me plenty if I had gone on and had it done.

Compression Testers

A compression tester is nothing but a pressure gauge. You insert it in the sparkplug hole in your block, turn the engine over so that you hit a minimum of four compression strokes, and read what the dial says. It's that simple.

The gauge reads in pounds per square inch, or psi. How

This is the least expensive type of compression tester. The rubber or neophrene tip is held in the sparkplug hole by brute force. On engines kicking out 200 psi (pounds per square inch) you may not be able to hold it in. Also, since this is a rigid unit, the tight fit of many engine compartments may make it impossible to get a unit like this into the hole.

much it should read is included in the tune-up data in your car's shop manual. It will vary with the automobile design and the engine's compression ratio.

You must turn the engine over at cranking speed to use the compression gauge. If you have a buddy who can sit in the driver's seat and turn the starter when you tell him, you are in great shape. If not, then you'll have to invest in a remote starter switch. Remote switches cost around $2.50 up. There is a button switch you push on one end. At the other end are two leads. One of these leads is clipped to the battery connection on the starter solenoid. The other goes to the starter lead wire. Then when you press the switch you bypass the ignition switch.

A word of caution: Don't use the remote starter switch any more than you must. Starters pull an enormous amount of current. It is easy to run your battery down.

If there is very little space so that you can't get into the plug hole with the rigid one-piece tester, then you get one with a long hose like this.

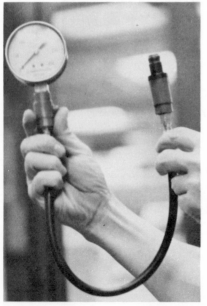

This shows a compression tester in action. This type has a screw base on the end of the hose to eliminate the difficulty of trying to hold the hand model in the hole against the heavy pressure of the engine's compression.

How to Check Compression

1. Remove all the sparkplugs from the cylinders. This will prevent the engine from starting when you press the starter button. First, however, run the engine to warm it to normal operating temperature.
2. Insert the compression tester in the Number 1 cylinder hole.
3. Turn the starter until the engine moves through at least four compression strokes. You can tell a compression stroke because the rising of the piston will cause the air/fuel mixture to rush out of the open sparkplug holes. You can hear the *whoosh* very distinctly. This air, remember, is fuel and is flammable.
4. The needle in the compression gauge dial will lock at its highest point until you release it by pushing a button on the side. The needle will give you the compression of the cylinder in pounds per square inch (psi). Write down the reading and the cylinder number. If you don't know how the cylinders are numbered, see Chapter 10, which covers cylinder numbers and how to determine the firing order of these cylinders.
5. After you check and record the reading of the number one cylinder, you do the same thing for number two and the rest of the cylinders in the engine.

How Much Should the Gauge Read?

How much the gauge should read varies with individual engines. *Engines,* that is, and not year models. Formerly, you could expect the psi specifications to remain fairly constant for several years, but the current emphasis on smog control has caused some manufacturers to lower the compression ratios of their engines. Thus you may not get as high a reading on a late-model car as you will on an earlier model.

The correct psi for your engine will be found in the shop manual for your model car or in the standard specification booklet you can get for about a dollar at most automobile supply houses.

If you can't get the specs for some reason, you should take a comparison test. That is, take a reading from all your cylinders. Take the highest reading cylinder as your base. If any of the other cylinders test out more than 25 percent lower than this, something is wrong in the engine.

Suppose one or more cylinders do test far below specs. Then what? If two side-by-side cylinders test about the same percent below the others, you can suspect a blown head gasket. This is the gasket between the cylinder head and the block. Compression is leaking out through the hole in the gasket. You'll need to have a new gasket put in.

If only one cylinder is bad, then mechanics suggest you put a spoonful of clean engine oil in the cylinder. Let the oil run down around the edges of the piston inside. Then retest the compression. If the reading improves, then this is a sign you have bad rings. (What happens is that the oil works as a temporary seal to keep the fuel from blowing past the worn rings.)

On the other hand, if the oil treatment in the cylinder does not cause the compression reading to rise, then you probably have bad valves. In either case, you need a motor overhaul.

Incidentally, if the oil test indicates that your rings are bad, try one of the oil additives that loosen stuck rings before you rush down to the garage to get new rings installed. Sometimes the poor compression is caused by rings getting jammed in their grooves by carbon, sludge, and varnishes. These oil additives, which you just pour into your crankcase as you would a new quart of oil, may be able to loosen up the stuck rings. If so, you are saved an expensive repair job. The additive will help only with stuck rings. It can't help if your rings are badly worn or if the cylinder is out of round from piston slap.

Compression Specs

You get your specs from your specification sheet, but here are a few common ones to give you some idea of how they vary from engine to engine.

Make	Year	Compression, psi
American Motors, 232	1971	180–190, with no more than 10 percent difference between cylinders.
Buick	1973	Lowest-reading cylinder
Chevrolet, all 6-cylinder models	1969–1964	130
Chevrolet, V8-427 and 350	1969–1968	160
Chrysler, 383 cu in., 2 bbl	1968	125–155
Ford, all models	1972	Lowest cylinder should not be more than 20 percent lower than the highest cylinder.
Plymouth, 361 cu in., 2-bbl	1966	125–155
Pontiac, 400	1970	185–210

On older cars that you bought secondhand you may find that factory specs don't work out right. This can sometimes be caused by the engine having been rebored. Reboring means that larger or oversize pistons had to be placed in the larger hole. Since the cubic inch displacement of an engine is the total volume of the cylinders, any reboring will change the total cubes of the engine.

Cylinders might get rebored because a hot-rod fan wanted increased compression, or because of a worn cylinder or scored cylinder walls.

Another thing that can upset your spec figures is engine swapping. If someone down the line changed engines in the car before you bought it, you have to know what the engine model is before you can get the correct specs. I know one owner who couldn't figure out what model engine he had under the hood, but he knew it wasn't the original engine. He asked around, but nobody he knew could tell him. So he borrowed a Polaroid camera, took a picture of the engine, and sent it to the manufacturer. He got his answer.

Incidently, standard compression testers you buy for a few dollars at your auto supply store only work on piston engines. They will not work on the Wankel (Mazda) rotary engine.

Chapter 5

THE COIL: ADDING A KICK

With the battery, compression and eyeball check behind us, we are now ready to follow the electricity through to the sparkplugs. As mentioned earlier when discussing batteries, all car batteries today put out 12 volts, volts being the *pressure* behind the current. However, it is necessary to have around 20,000 volts to get enough steam behind the current to give it the strength to leap across the gap at the terminals of the sparkplugs. It is this fire surging through the gas mixture between the terminals that ignites the fuel in the cylinder.

Something must cause this increase, and that something is the *coil*. The coil can be recognized as a small cylinder with one heavy wire running from the top center to the car's distributor. A small wire (called the primary circuit wire) runs from a terminal on one side of the coil, while a second wire connects to the other side terminal. A coil may be mounted with the high-tension terminal pointed up or down, but for the purpose of discussion we will call the top of the coil the end that the high-tension wire comes out of on its way to the distributor.

The coil is usually mounted somewhere close to the distributor. On V-8s this is generally on top between the two banks of cylinders. It may be in the front or back. Six-cylinder cars usually have them mounted either with a bracket to the side of the engine block or on the firewall close to the block. Coils can be ruined by excessive heat, and the farther they are removed from the engine and its heat the better for coil life. Much of coil failures come from heat, so it is a good idea to keep the coil clean. A heavy layer of dirt and grease on the coil housing can act as an insulation against air that would keep the coil cool. Dirt can also cause a short between the terminals.

An Ignition Team

It is necessary to consider the coil and the distributor to-gether, because they work as a team. There are two electrical circuits in the coil. One has a 12-volt battery current flowing through it. The second is the one that carries our stepped-up high-tension current to the spark plug.

The total ignition system consists of the following:
- *The battery*—source of the current.
- An *ammeter* or charging light—to show whether the bat-tery is charging or discharging.
- An *ignition switch.* Current will not flow from the battery until it has a complete circuit to flow from the positive to the negative terminal. The switch breaks the circuit when it is *off* and completes the circuit when it is *on.*
- A *ballast resistor* (not on all cars). The ballast resistor is in the circuit to permit a full battery jolt to the starter, but also to cut down voltage not needed by the rest of the ignition system. It rarely causes trouble, and many tune-up manu-als don't even bother to mention it.
- The *ignition coil*—to step up the 12-volt current to the required firing voltage, generally from 18,000 to 24,000 volts.
- *The distributor*—to do exactly what its name implies: distribute the high-tension current provided by the coil to the individual sparkplugs *at the right time.*

• And finally the *sparkplugs,* which may be considered the car's "matches," for their job is to set the fuel on fire.

The plugs are grounded to the block and the block to the frame, so that the car's frame serves as the final link in the ignition chain to complete the electrical circuit needed to cause current to flow through the system.

Inside the Coil

Nobody really knows what electricity is. Scientists have a theory that they think explains it as a flow or exchange of charged particles, but it remains incomplete because of various inconsistencies.

However, we do know how it acts. One of the things we know is that if an electrical conducting wire is wrapped around

This shows the coil-distributor arrangement on a V-8 engine. Here they are in the front. A is the coil. B is the distributor cap. C is the high tension coil wire going from the center tower of the coil to the center tower of the distributor. D is the primary circuit terminal to which the primary wire G is attached to connect the coil with the points in the distributor. F is the battery wire terminal and E is the wire leading to the battery.

a core of soft iron and a current is sent through the wire, a magnetic field will be created around the iron core. In other words, if you wrap some copper wire around a rod of soft iron, you make an electromagnet. This magnetic field will last only as long as the current of electricity flows through the wire.

This electromagnet differs from a permanent iron magnet in that the latter keeps its magnetism. The electromagnet is the heart of the coil and is very important to us in tune-up work.

Inside the coil is a soft iron core, which is wrapped with several turns of wire in order to make an electromagnet in the coil. This is the coil's *primary winding*. This winding has no other purpose than to create a magnetic field in the coil. The current coming from the battery into the coil and running through this *primary circuit* never reaches the sparkplugs.

The accompanying diagram shows the current's path. The juice from the battery comes in through the wire *A* and passes through the *primary windings* of the coil *B,* continuing through the primary circuit *C,* out the terminal and through the wire *D* into the *side* of the distributor, where the current flows through the *closed* points *E* and to the ground *F* to complete the circuit.

The sole purpose of this current is to create a strong electro-magnetic effect in the primary windings. This in turn creates a strong magnetic field around the primary windings. This current is 12 volts, or whatever your battery is putting out.

Before going on to explain why we are so anxious to get a strong magnetic field in the coil, we had better pause a moment to talk about the points. Everybody who does tune-up work talks about points. In fact, if more drivers thought about their points there would be less cars stopping in the middle of the road. Changing the points is one of the basic operations in tune-up work. And by "points" we *don't* mean the sparkplugs.

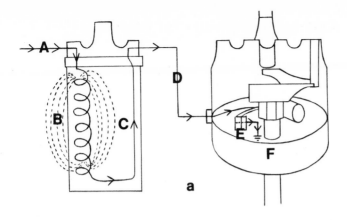

a

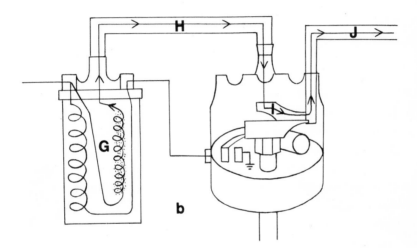

b

Here is how the primary and secondary circuits work in the coil and distributor. Battery current A enters the coil and passes through the large windings to make a strong magnetic field B. The current then passes on through the primary wire C to the distributor where it flows through the closed contact points D. The current then goes through the ground to return to the battery. This diagram shows only the primary circuit in the coil. The secondary circuit was removed in the drawing for clarity.

In the second drawing (b), the secondary circuit has been added. Notice that the contact points in the distributor are now open. No current flows in the primary circuit. When the points opened, the magnetic field (B in the top drawing) collapsed. The collapsing magnetic field cut across the fine windings of the secondary circuit E, inducing a voltage as high as 25,000 volts. This high-tension current flows through the high-tension coil wire F to the center terminal tower of the distributor where it passes through the contacts on the rotor G to the distributor cap insert and then to the sparkplug wire H to go to the sparkplug. The spinning rotor touches each of the inserts (one for every cylinder) to send firing current to each in turn.

What the Points Are For

The points—correctly, contact points—are two round pieces of metal attached to a spring and a rubbing block. The spring holds them closed until the rubbing block, riding against the cam in the center of the distributor, pushes them open.

As we have said, the current from one terminal of the battery flows through the primary winding of the coil, setting up a strong magnetic field inside the coil, then flows through the primary circuit wire into the side of the distributor, passing through the points and then to the ground to return to the other terminal of the battery.

The points act as a switch to stop the primary circuit when the breaker cam in the center of the distributor pushes the points apart.

The high magnetic field in the coil, caused by electricity flowing through the primary wiring around the soft iron core, collapses when the current is cut off. Opening the points breaks the circuit so that the current no longer flows through the primary wiring.

When the magnetic field collapses, the magnetic lines of force cut across the fine wiring of the secondary wiring. It hits with such a jolt that it kicks the low pressure 12-volt juice up to as much as 20,000 to 25,000 volts, depending upon the engine design.

This high-tension current flows through the center tower terminal of the coil and through the coil wire to the center tower of the distributor.

What Happens in the Distributor?

Let's follow the new action in another diagram. It looks pretty much like the one we used for explaining the primary circuit. But notice in this second diagram that the points are open. This means that the primary circuit we discussed before

When the rubbing block pushes against the lobe of the distributor cam, the points (indicated by arrow) are pushed open. This breaks the primary circuit, inducing a high voltage in the secondary circuit, which provides the 20,000 volts necessary to jump the spark gap.

is now dead. Its strong magnetic field of force has collapsed, hit the secondary wiring in the coil X with a jolt sufficient to kick the voltage up to the required amount to jump a sparkplug gap.

This is the inside of a distributor with the rotor removed. This type of distributor has the centrifugal advance weights under the breaker plate. The parts are: A, breaker plate; B, primary wire; C, breaker points; D, Condenser; F, connection joining condenser wire to the primary circuit; G, ground wire; H, breaker cam. The rubbing block is the small rectangular piece in the center of the breaker points arm, pressing against the cam. It is very easy to change points and condenser on this type of distributor. It requires only disconnecting the condenser and primary wires and removing two screws in the breaker point set and one screw holding the condenser.

This high-tension current flows up through the the coil's center tower and through the coil wire *Y* to the center tower of the distributor.

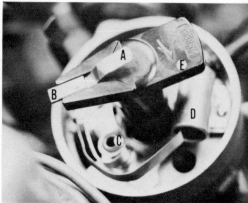

The path of the high-tension coil electricity can be followed in these illustrations as it goes through the distributor. The left-hand picture shows the all-weather plastic cap removed from the distributor. The right-hand picture shows the uncovered distributor with the rotor E in place.

The high-tension juice from the coil comes through the distributor cap to the carbon button A (left picture) and makes contact with the rotor conductor at A in the right photo. The current passes along this conductor to the rotor tip B which, as it removes, makes contact with the inserts (B, left picture) that protrude from each of the towers to which the individual spark plug wires are attached. The revolving rotor touches each of the inserts in turn to send the high tension current to the plugs. Items marked C and D in the distributor are the point set and the condenser.

The current then flows through the distributor cap, and a contact in the bottom of the cap passes the current to a conductor mounted on the distributor rotor. As the rotor spins, it touches inserts in the distributor cap. These inserts contact the individual sparkplug wires that carry the surge of high-tension current to the sparkplugs to fire the cylinders.

Magnetic force must build up in the coil and the magnetic field must collapse each time a sparkplug fires. When your engine is idling at 500 revolutions per minute (rpm), this build-up and collapse may occur 125 times a minute. But on the road at 4,000 rpm, the build up and collapse may be 1,000 times a minute—or more, depending on the number of cylinders.

Checking the Coil

The coil is sealed and cannot be repaired. You replace it if it is faulty. Testing it requires instruments. However, one of the oldest ways to test an ignition system is to remove a sparkplug wire with the engine idling. Hold the metal terminal of the wire close to a clean portion of the metal block. A spark will jump from the wire to the block. If this spark is fat and blue, you're okay in your ignition. A weak spark indicates trouble *somewhere*. (If the protecting boot is molded on the wire and you can't push it back to expose the wire sufficiently to get a spark, then insert a piece of conductor metal into the end of the wire.)

This test tells you only whether the system as a whole is working or not. If you're not showing a good spark, the trouble can be anything from a poor battery to corroded points or poor wiring. You have to use elimination to decide which it is. Check your battery, wires, connections and distributor circuit, including points. If they all check out okay, there's nothing left but the coil.

Another no-cost way to check a coil, often recommended, is temporarily to replace the suspected coil with one known to be good from another car. If it runs right, then you know your coil is defective.

This is all very fine, but substituting coils has its drawbacks too. Coils come in different strengths to fit different ignition systems. Before you borrow a coil from another of the family's cars or from a friend, be sure its capacity fits your car. You'll have to check the manufacturer's specs to find out.

Also, depending upon the cause of the coil failure, some coils work okay when they are cold and fail when they warm up. You have to look out for this also. Test at normal operating temperature.

Checking over an auto parts catalog current in 1973, I see a coil tester listed for $5.98 that is guaranteed (so the ad says) to tell you whether the coil is good, bad, or shorted. Well, $5.98 (plus sales tax, I suppose) isn't much. But when you add another six bucks to the price of battery terminal cleaners, battery testers, ohmmeters, voltmeters, offset tools to reach the distributor hold-down bolts, ignition wrenches, and umpteen other little things that don't cost much in themselves, you wind up shelling out a mint. If you are going into tune-up as a business or a semibusiness, this is fine. You need all this stuff, if for no other reason than that they cut down your working time tremendously. For the backyarder who is only going to tune his own bus every few months, you're probably better off —at least financially—to do a lot of the work the hard way while you gradually assemble the tools you could use to advantage.

Summing Up

As a general rule you'll find that coils are pretty rugged. You'll not have much trouble with them. If you have weak or no spark, check the rest of the ignition system before you begin worrying about the coil.

Many beginning mechanics find automotive electricity confusing. A thorough knowledge of all phases of the electrical system is highly desirable, for you'll have less trouble trying to decide what is wrong if you know what every part of your engines does and why it does it.

However, if you are one of those who has trouble with figuring out all the ins and outs of the electrical system, for home tune-ups you don't really have to remember that the primary circuit of the coil forms a "saturated" magnetic field of force that cuts across the primary windings of the coil when the field collapses due to opening points.

Just remember these facts:

- The 12-volt current from the battery is not strong enough to jump the spark gap and ignite the fuel in the cylinder.
- So we have a coil. Its job is to take the 12-volt current and give it a kick so that it becomes strong enough to jump the spark gap. This kick can be as much as 20,000 to 25,000 volts. The higher a car's compression, the greater must be the voltage to jump the gap. This is because the higher compression packs fuel tighter into the cylinder. It is harder for the spark to get through the tighter-packed fuel, and therefore it needs more push (voltage) behind it.
- If a coil goes bad, it cannot be repaired. It must be replaced. Replacing a coil is simple. Unscrew the two leads (from the battery and to the distributor), unscrew or pull out, as the need may be, the high-tension wire to the distributor central tower. Then loosen the bracket holding the coil to the engine or firewall. That's all there is to it.

CAUTION: All electrical systems must be arranged according to correct *polarity*. Correct polarity means getting the negative and positive poles right, or connecting positive terminals to positive terminals, negative terminals to negative terminals. In electrical currents the juice flows from negative to positive— and if you reverse this polarity, you are in trouble. So if you remove a coil for checking or to replace it, be sure you put it back the same way it went on.

Check List for Coil Service

1. Check terminals for loose wires. Tighten if necessary.
2. Clean oil and grease and dirt accumulations from coil housing.
3. Check wiring for frayed or cracked insulation. Replace wiring if necessary.
4. Check coil with coil tester if available.
5. Check high-tension terminal tower for cracks.

6. Remove high-tension wire. In some coils the wire terminal is inserted directly into the tower and held in place by friction and a rubber boot over the outside for protection. In other models the protective cap on the tower is plastic and screws onto the tower.

7. With the high-tension wire removed from the tower, inspect the terminal of the wire and the insert in the tower. Look for evidence of burning or fusing. If the high-tension wire is not inserted fully and firmly in the tower, it can cause a gap that forces the high-tension current from the coil to arc across the gap. Arcing can build up carbon, causing resistance that can lower the voltage or even bring about a complete electrical failure. After the terminals are cleaned, be sure that you press the wires firmly back in place.

8. Any time a sparkplug wire is removed while the engine is running, it should be grounded. Grounding means giving the current some place to go. You can ground an ignition wire by clipping a jumper wire to it and connecting the other end to the engine block or to the body frame. Failure to ground ignition wires causes a build-up of voltage in the coil. This high-tension current has no place to go and can lead to premature coil failure. And you can also get a nasty shock if you touch the wire while you yourself are grounded to the car or to earth.

Chapter 6

MYSTERIES OF THE DISTRIBUTOR

There is something mysterious about a distributor that frightens many beginners. Actually an automobile distributor is simple in its actions and simple to work on. It is the only element of the entire ignition system that has any mechanical action. The battery, the coil, the ballast resistor, and the sparkplugs have no moving parts. (The starter and the starter solenoid are moving parts, of course, but we are not considering them as part of the ignition system. The ignition system is that subassembly of the car that is concerned with making a spark at the electrodes of the sparkplug.)

In the preceding chapter on coils we explained what happens to the battery electricity in the distributor, but it might be well to summarize it again quickly:

- The battery's 12-volt current flows through the primary circuit in the coil and from the coil to the contact points in the distributor.
- This current, whose only job is to build a magnetic field in the coil, continues to flow as long as the contact points are closed.
- The contact points are nothing but a switch which opens and closes to break the primary circuit so that the collaps-

ing magnetic field can induce a high-tension current in the secondary circuit.

• This high-tension current goes out the top tower of the coil and into the central tower of the distributor cap. It makes contact with a rotor that turns inside the distributor to pass the pulse of high-tension current to the proper sparkplug wire at the proper time.

Distributor Types

There are basically three types of distributors you'll come in contact with. They all do the same thing but employ different ways to do it.

One type, illustrated in the accompanying picture, is the standard rotor type with the centrifugal advance under the breaker plate. The breaker plate is the movable piece of metal the points and condenser are attached to. The centrifugal advance are a set of weights mounted below the breaker plate. When the shaft of the distributor picks up sufficient speed, these weights are swung out by centrifugal force. This is the same principle that makes a pail of water on a rope keep from spilling when slung around by a boy. The movement of these weights causes the breaker plate to move. That changes the timing of the car, making the sparkplugs fire a bit earlier than they do when the car is idling.

The second type, illustrated in the accompanying exploded drawing, works exactly like the type described above but has its parts in a different place. In this distributor, used by General Motors and on some American Motors cars, a circular rotor and the centrifugal advance mechanism are mounted above the breaker points and condenser. A unique feature of this distributor is its "peek-a-boo" window in the side which permits adjustment of the breaker point gap while the engine is running and the distributor cap in place.

The third type of distributor is one you don't see much. It

This shows one end of a camshaft. The lobes on the camshaft open and close the valves to let fuel into the cylinders and exhaust out, but the slanting gear, indicated by the arrow, connects with a similar gear at the bottom of the distributor shaft. This drives the breaker cam and the rotor in the distributor.

Spring clips (indicated by arrow) hold the cap on this Chrysler distributor. They are pushed aside and the distributor cap lifted off. This exposes the rotor, points, and condenser for easy checking and replacement. In this type distributor, the contrifugal advance weights are out of sight, under the breaker plate.

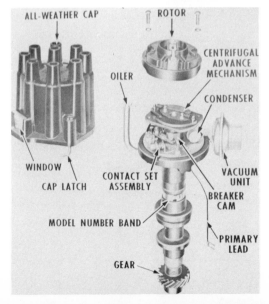

This type of distributor, used on General Motors cars and some American Motors cars, has a circular rotor with the centrifugal advance mechanism mounted above the breaker plate with its contact points and condenser. Although it looks quite different from the distributor with the centrifugal advance hidden under the breaker plate, it works in exactly the same manner.

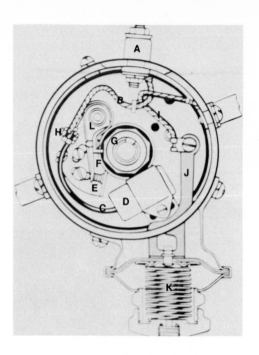

is the electronic transistor type. It is unique in having no points to set or burn and no condenser to give trouble. This type of distributor has been around for a while. Several companies have experimented with it and some have used it as optional equipment. Chrysler, in 1972, was the first company to make a transistor distributor standard equipment on a stock car.

The Components of a Distributor

Up to this point our discussion of the distributor has centered on how the primary circuit electricity flows through the distributor and how the points open and close to switch the current on and off. There are other very important functions of the distributor.

Referring to the attached diagram of a typical standard rotor distributor with centrifugal advance system under the breaker plate, we have the following parts: *A,* connection to the primary wire from the coil; *B,* wire from connection *A* to connector *H,* where the primary circuit wire attaches to the condenser wire *C* leading to condenser *D*. *L* is the contact points spring assembly, *F* the rubbing block that rides against cam *G*. *Letter E* indicates the breaker points, which are closed in this drawing, showing that the primary circuit is flowing. *J* is the operating arm for the vacuum advance and *K* the vacuum advance itself. *I* is a ground wire.

The Electrical Path

Now, going back to *A* where the current enters the distributor, the 12-volt primary current flows through the wire *B* to the connection *H* and then turns upward along the breaker-point spring through the breaker-point arm to the points. When the breaker points, *E*, open, the current that has been flowing to the points stops, and the condenser *D* absorbs the current through the wire *C* to keep the current from trying to jump the points gap. This collapses the magnetic field in the coil, inducing the hot spark needed for the plugs.

The other item of interest in this diagram of the inside of the distributor is the cam *G*. The rotor, which rides on top of the cam and rotates with the shaft, has been removed in order to clearly show details. Notice that there are eight flat sides on the cam, creating eight points or lobes, and indicating that this particular distributor is made for an eight-cylinder engine.

How the Distributor Cam Works

If the distributor was for a six-cylinder engine there would be only six lobes and only four for a four-cylinder engine.

The rubbing block *F* is a permanent part of the breaker arm. One end rides against the cam. As the cam turns, the high lobe pushes against the rubbing block, which in turn pushes the points open.

The vacuum advance *K* and its operating arm *J* work in connection with the hidden centrifugal advance to change the timing of the spark at different automobile speeds. We'll forget them for the moment, returning to them when we talk about timing an engine—an essential part of engine tune-up.

Things to Check for Distributor Tune-up

We have now finished explaining how things operate and are ready to start actual work on the distributor. First of all we'll make a check list.

1. Remove each sparkplug wire from the cap *one at a time* and inspect the wire and its terminal for evidence of burning, cracks, or frayed insulation. You can use an inexpensive test light or continuity tester to check for breaks in the conductor. An ohmmeter, which checks resistance, should be used if available. Replace each wire *one at a time,* after checking, in the same hole it came from. If you *do* remove more than one wire at a time and forget where each goes, refer to Chapter 10 where we talk about the firing order of plugs. Strange things can happen when you get your wires mixed up. You might even ruin your engine.

2. Check the plastic distributor cap for cracks, broken towers, or carbon tracks (evidence of shorts) and replace the cap if necessary.

3. Check the inside as well as the outside of the distributor cap. The cap is removed on some models by flipping down two spring catches on the sides. On GM peek-a-boo distributors there are two crossheaded screws on opposite sides of the distributor cap. Turn them with a crosspoint screwdriver. The screws have a catch at the bottom and a half-turn unlocks them. It is not necessary to remove the sparkplug wires when you take the cap off. Inside look for carbon tracks, burned inserts, grease, and dirt. Clean thoroughly.

4. Remove the rotor. The GM circular rotor is held on by two screws. Loosen them and lift the rotor up. On other

This shows the centrifugal advance mechanism mounted on top of the distributor. As the shaft spins, weights A and B move out, which causes the engine timing to advance.

types the rotor is held to the distributor shaft by friction. All you do to remove it is pull straight up. There is a lip on the rotor that fits into an opening on the shaft so you can't put it back wrong. Inspect the rotor for a tight fit on the shaft and for evidence of burning at the contact points.

5. Inspect the connections to see that the primary wire and the condenser wire are tight.
6. Check the points by pushing them open. Look for burning, pitting and excessive transfer of metal.
7. Check the rubbing block for signs of wear.
8. If everything is in good shape, then all you have to do is check the points for correct gap and dwell and replace the cap. How to do this will be explained in the next chapter.

Since it is highly unlikely that you will find the points and dwell in good shape, the next step is to replace the contact points assembly and the condenser. There was a time when mechanics recommended that you file the contact points, but today's tungsten points don't file very well. Since a tune-up kit (containing a points set, condenser and new rotor) costs only from about $1.50 to $6 depending on the car, number of cylinders, and quality of the set, you will relieve yourself of a lot of future trouble by replacing all of them.

Replacing the Points

Opinions differ on whether you should remove the distributor from the automobile or not when you work on it. It is easier to work on the distributor if it is removed and taken to a work bench. And it is easy to remove and simple to reinstall—*if* you know how. Otherwise it can be a frustrating mess and you may find that you can't start your car when you put back the distributor. For this reason we recommend that you do not try to remove the distributor until you have gained more experience.

We would recommend that until you gain practice in working inside a distributor you use locking tools. These will prevent your dropping screws and nuts. Some distributor plates have holes in them for making adjustments. If you drop a screw down one of them, you have a problem getting it out.

Tools for Changing Points

1. Screwdrivers of a size to fit. Some screws may be cross-point headed on certain distributors.
2. A set of small ignition wrenches. These will be used to loosen the nut sometimes used to hold together the terminals of the condenser wire and the primary current wire. The wrenches may also be needed to tighten the connector on the side of the distributor.

In addition to these few tools, you'll need a tune-up kit. Be sure that you get one for your specific car.

Removing Points and Condenser

You must first remove the primary current-carrying wire and the condenser wire. The point where the two leads join is marked with an *H* in the diagram of the inside of the distributor. The two leads end in flat, slotted terminals. Carefully note the way they come off and that the two terminals are mounted *back-to-back.*

How they are mounted varies with different makes of distributors. On the GE Chevrolet window-type distributor illustrated here, the two terminals are held together by the screw marked with the arrow. All you have to do is loosen this screw and slide the slotted terminals up. Note that on this particular model the primary wire and the condenser wire run parallel, with the condenser wire terminal on the inside.

On the other hand, in the photograph of the older-type distributor, with the centrifugal advance underneath, the two

The circular plastic rotor on the GM window type of distributor is removed by loosening two screw bolts, indicated by arrows. Tip A contacts the inserts in the distributor head and point B contacts the insert connecting with the high-tension wire from the coil. It can be seen that although this cap differs in appearance from the slender rotor in the other type of distributors, it is identical in actual operation.

terminals are held together by a nut on a bolt that extends through the contact points spring. Loosen the nut and pull the two contacts up and out. Put them back the same way. Always observe carefully how you remove them and and you'll have no trouble putting them back. Observe which of the two is on top and that they must be mounted back to back.

If you do this, you'll have no trouble even when you are working on distributors that vary somewhat from these two examples.

Incidentally, in some of the Chrysler pretransistor distributors, there is no wire to the condenser. Instead they use a thin band of flat copper, which amounts to the same thing. Consider and treat it as a wire and go about your work.

Removing the Contact Points Assembly

After the two screws are removed, it is necessary only to pick up the contact points assembly. In the type known as the preassembled set (like the one shown in the accompanying photograph) the points, rubbing block, breaker arm, spring and contact junction for the electrical leads are all mounted on a small metal base. It is picked up and moved as a unit.

The contact points assembly on the window-type distributors looks somewhat different from this one, but it is also removed as a unit by loosening two set screws.

There is another type of assembly in which the set of points comes off in two sections, but basically both types are about the same. The important thing is to remember how you took them off, so you can put them back on in the same manner when you put in the new points.

Putting in the New Points

Some of the tune-up kits come with illustrated directions, but these are not necessary. Just take the new condenser and screw it tightly in place, but don't connect the condenser wire

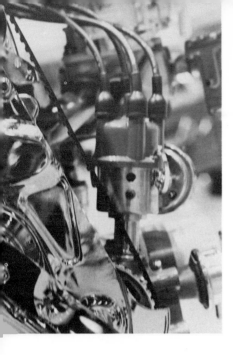

The number of towers on a distributor equal the number of cylinders in the engine plus one. The extra tower is for the high-tension wire from the coil. This is the distributor used on a Pinto.

yet. Depending on the type of distributor, the wire might get in your way when you put in the points.

Next, take a careful look at the bottom of the base plate of the points assembly. On most types you'll see a small pin, which must fit into a small hole you'll find between the two screw holes in the distributor breaker plate. The purpose of this is to help you align the points in the right position. When you put in the points be sure that the ground wire is connected. Screw down the holding screws tightly to give good contact.

Next, connect up the two leads. Remember that they go back-to-back in the same manner that they came off. If the condenser contact was on top and the primary wire contact on the bottom, put them back that way.

And that is all there is to *taking out* the old points and putting in new ones. Now comes the job of adjusting new points. This is not difficult but it is very important. Failure to adjust the points may cause you more trouble than if you had left the old burned points in the distributor.

What to Do

Before dealing in detail with each specific action, let's list the things that have to be done:

1. Check alignment of the points.
2. Check the tension of the spring.
3. Check and set the points gap.
4. And/or set the "dwell."

On this distributor, used on older Fords, it is necessary only to loosen three screws to remove both points and condenser. Removing screws A and B permits lifting the points assembly out. The condenser is held by a single screw C. The flat, slotted terminals generally used in distributors are shown at D. This is the primary circuit wire. It and a similar terminal from the condenser wire are mounted back to back and slipped down at E between the contact points spring and the nut shown here. To remove it the nut is loosened and the terminals lifted out. To put them back in, slip the two flat terminals in between the spring and the nut. Then tighten the nut with a small ignition wrench. In this distributor, unlike the window-type illustrated previously, the two wires do not lie parallel. They circle the inside of the distributor from opposite directions and meet at the connection junction. If you carefully observe these details when you dismount points and condenser you will have no trouble reassembling any of the different types.

The screw holding the condenser and primary circuit wires in contact with the contact points connection on the Chevrolet GM window-type distributor is marked with the arrow. Loosen this screw and the slotted terminals can be slid upward.

On this type of distributor it is necessary only to remove two screws and then the points set can be lifted out of the distributor. The old set is thrown away, replaced by a new set.

5. Lubricate the cam.
6. Install new rotor.

Checking Point Alignment

Some points sets require no alignment, according to the manufacturers. American Motors, for example, say their preassembled sets require no alignment or adjusting of the tension spring. It is best to check anyway. Sometimes little errors can get past the company inspectors.

Alignment means the way the two faces of the points come together. They should come together squarely. The faces should not be above or below each other, nor should they meet at an angle. Modern tungsten points are not flat but are slightly curved. You do not try to file them flat as was formerly the practice. Never file points. The slight curve will not hurt. Just insure that the two faces met squarely in the center.

And if they don't? One face of the points is mounted to the breaker arm. Let it alone. The other face is mounted solidly to the base plate. Bend this one gently with a pair of thin long-nose pliers until the two faces are in alignment. *Never try to bend the breaker arm.*

On this Ford distributor a single screw holds the condenser in place. In contrast, the Chrysler condenser was held by a metal band around the condenser and the band was fastened to the breaker plate by two screws at the side.

Spring Tension

The spring tension is very important. This spring has two functions. It holds the points closed and it presses the rubbing block snugly against the cam. If the tension is too tight, it will cause premature wear of the rubbing block, which in turn will upset the spark-gap adjustment. If the tension is too loose, it will not hold the points tightly closed during the time the primary circuit current flow is building up the magnetic field in the coil. At high speeds a spring tension that is too weak can cause the points to "bounce." This bouncing back open before the coil magnetic field has reached its design peak (that is, before it has become "saturated") can cause a miss in the engine because the high-tension potential has not been reached.

A weak spring will also fail to hold the rubbing block firmly against the cam, resulting in a current-flow variation.

Checking Breaker-Arm Spring Tension

A spring gauge is used to check spring tension. This gauge works exactly like a pair of spring scales. As shown in the accompanying photograph, one end is hooked over the point on the breaker arm. Then you pull back until the points just begin to open. At this point you read the gauge. The reading is in ounces of pull. The amount it should read is fairly standard through one make of cars, but varies from make to make. Here are recommended spring tension readings for some of the more popular cars for the past ten years.

Make	Year		Spring Tension, psi
American Motors (incl. Rambler)	1973–1964		17–21
Buick	1973–1964		19–23
Cadillac			19–23
Chevrolet			19–23
Chrysler			17–20 (although some models can go up to 21½)
Cougar, Comet			17–21
Corvette			19–23 (except 1969, 1968 427, which is 28–32)
Dodge			17–21
Ford			17–21 except the following:
	1967	427	22–24
	1966	427	22–24
	1966	Mustang 289 4-bbl *high perf*	27–30
	1965	Galaxie and custom 427 4bbl	27–30
	1964	223, 200, 170 Fairlane	17–20
	1964	Galaxie 427	27–30
	1964	Galaxie 390 289, 352, 260	17–20
	1964	Fairlane 289 4-bbl	27–30
Oldsmobile			19–23
Plymouth			17–20 (although a few models recommend 17–21½
Pontiac			19–23

If the points do not align correctly, bend the stationary support and not the breaker arm to mate the points squarely. Use thin nose pliers and bend gently the part indicated by the arrow. Never bend the breaker arm.

How to Adjust Spring Tension

New models may be preset, meaning there is no way you can change the tension. If the breaker arm doesn't test at the correct tension, then you take it back for an exchange. Some older models have a slot in the end of the spring where it fits over the insulated post to contact with the coil and primary wire. (The three join because the spring serves as a conductor to carry the current from the junction to the points.) You adjust the spring tension by moving the spring forward to increase tension, and backward (which makes the loop larger around the pivot post of the spring) to decrease tension.

Now that the spring tension has been checked, we can move on to the problem of adjusting the points. This involves such things as breaker-points gap and dwell—two vital factors in tune-up.

The tension of the distributor spring is tested with a special spring gauge. One end of gauge is hooked over the point face on the movable arm. Then the gauge is pulled backward until the points just begin to open. Note the reading at this point.

Chapter 7

GAP AND DWELL

Once the new points are installed, they must be gapped, and-/or have their dwell adjusted. The "gap" refers to how wide the points are pushed open by the lobe of the cam pressing on the rubbing block. The "dwell" indicates how long the points stay closed between openings. Dwell (points closed) is the time needed for the magnetic field to build up in the coil. If the dwell isn't long enough, the spark doesn't have enough time to build up to full intensity. The dwell is the more important of the two, for the gap size merely governs the dwell time.

For example, the wider you make the gap, the shorter the dwell between openings will be. In the same manner, a smaller gap gives us a longer dwell. Adjusting either one changes the other.

You adjust both in the same manner. That is, you loosen the set screw on the points set when the rubbing block is resting on the tip of the cam lobe. Then you move the points farther apart or closer to get the right specs. This adjusts both gap and dwell. Why do we talk about adjusting gap *or* dwell when we're doing both at the same time? The difference is in which one we *measure* while doing our adjusting.

You measure gap by inserting a feeler gauge between the

points at full gap. Dwell is measured with an electronic dwell meter, which can be bought from $10 up. A good tach/dwell meter can be had for $20 up, enabling you to use it both for setting the points and for checking rpm when you set your carburetor. If you can set the gap with a fifty-cent feeler gauge, why shell out for a dwell meter? Once all points sets were set with a feeler gauge. It was all that was available. But as points age they burn and pit—the surface of the contacts is no longer smooth. A flat gauge blade measures only from the high spots on the two surfaces. It does not give a true gap reading. Dwell, which is measured electronically from the split second the current is interrupted until it begins again, is much more exact. Provided, of course, that the meter is accurate. Some of the cheaper ones aren't always right.

What Dwell Really is

Dwell is measured in degrees of a circle. The cam in your distributor makes a complete circle, or 360 degrees. If you have a six-cylinder car, there are six lobes and six flat surfaces on the cam in your distributor. Similarly, if you have a four-cylinder car there are four, and on an eight-cylinder car there are eight. Going back to our six-cylinder car, we divide our six cylinders into the 360 degrees that the distributor cam turns for one complete firing of all cylinders and obtain 60 degrees for each single cylinder. This means that the dwell (closed time) and the gap (open time) for each cylinder must add up to 60 degrees (see diagram). If you have an eight-cylinder car, you are going to have to build up and collapse your magnetic field with only 45 degrees per cylinder.

Our problem is, how many of those degrees do we give the dwell? Or how long can we keep the points closed so we can get a fully saturated magnetic field in the coil? The answer is in the spec sheet you'll find in the technical manual of your car or in the $1 spec sheet chart you can get at any auto supply

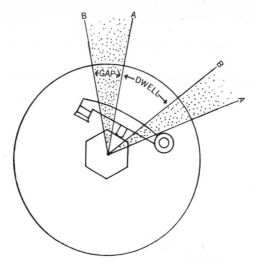

A *is the point on the cam when the lobe of the cam first pushes the point* apart. B *is the point on the cam where the points close. While only a single dwell and two gaps are shown here, there is a dwell for each flat surface of the cam and a gap for each lobe. There are six for a six-cylinder car, eight for an eight-cylinder car, and four for a four-cylinder car—one for each sparkplug.*

house. This same spec chart will also have the gap setting, if you prefer to go that route instead of using a dwell meter. Just to give a general idea, here are some of the gap/dwell settings on a few of the better known cars:

Make	Year	Gap	Dwell	Model
American Motors	1972	.016	32°	232 cu in.
			32°	256 cu in.
			30°	All others
Chevrolet	1972	.019	32°	140–250 cu in.
			30°	All others
Ford	1972	.017	28°	302 V-8
		.020	28°	351 V-8

Setting the Gap

There are three different ways to set the points gap, depending on what kind of distributor you have. Conventional distributors—the kind with the centrifugal advance mechanism under the breaker plate—may have the gap set in either of two ways. The accompanying photographs show the most common type. Note, as indicated by the arrow, the hole in the breaker plate. Observe that there is a tiny slot in one side of this hole and a similar slot in the edge of the base plate of the points assembly. Now if you loosen the screw marked *A* and then wedge a screwdriver blade so that it fits into the two slots, you can force the points open by twisting the screwdriver in a counterclockwise direction (on this particular distributor).

To adjust the gap to specs you tap the starter, causing the cam to turn until you have the rubbing block directly on top of the cam lobe. This will open the points to the largest gap permitted by the cam. Measure this gap by inserting a feeler gauge between the points. Suppose we have a 1972 Ford with a 351 V-8 engine. Looking back at our specs, we see that the gap should be .020. If it does not check out at this measurement, then open or close the gap by twisting the screwdriver counterclockwise to enlarge the gap and clockwise to close the gap until it has the correct gap. Then remove the screwdriver, tighten down the loosened screw so that the gap is locked in place. That's all there is to it.

You will occasionally find a distributor that is "backwards," as some turn clockwise and some counterclockwise. It makes no difference in adjusting. If you can't decide which way to twist to open and close the gap, just twist and watch. You won't hurt anything. If you go the wrong way, then twist the other way.

Remember of course that you should use this method of adjusting the gap only if you are putting in new points. If points are pitted badly or if there has been an excess transfer of metal from one set to the other, the rough surface will not permit you to get a true reading.

Don't File Your Points

There was a time when filing points to flatten them out again was standard service station practice. This doesn't work so well with modern hard tungsten points. You should replace the points when they get pitted. Depending on the car, you should be able to get yourself a tune-up kit with a set of points, a new rotor and a condenser for from $1.49 to $4.95. A new set of points, if you really needed them, will save you that much in gasoline.

Incidently, if your car sometimes stops on the road and you check and find that you're getting gas to the carburetor and the battery is still strong, take a look at your points. (You can tell that the battery is O.K. if the starter works.) Many times such stoppages are caused by points so badly burned that the primary current can't get through because of the resistance. This burning can be caused by a poor condenser, or by putting too much grease on the cam so that it gets on the points, where it burns. Running the car with the wrong-size gap can sometimes cause arcing, which also burns the points. On window-type distributors, not closing the window properly may permit dirt and oil to get in and burn the points also.

If you find that the points are burned and you're far from home or a service station, then you might try scraping the points with a pen knife to remove some of the corrosion or use an ignition file if you have one in your tool kit. You can usually remove enough burned matter to get a current through the points. This is only a temporary adjustment. The points should be replaced as quickly as possible.

Eccentric Screw Adjustment

If you inspect your distributor and do not find an adjustment hole and slot, then on the plate that holds the contact points set you will find a screw head in addition to the ones that

In the top photograph the arrows point to the adjusting hole in the breaker plate. First loosen the locking screw A, then insert a screwdriver blade into the hole. Be sure that it is of sufficient size to fit into the two small slots that you can see in the top picture. One is on the hole in the breaker plate and the other is on the base plate of the points set. The bottom photograph shows how the screwdriver blade fits into these slots. A is the locking screw which must be loosened before the points can be moved beyond their previous setting. This adjustment must be made with the rubbing block sitting directly on top of the cam lobe. In the bottom photo the condenser wire has been removed so it would not obscure detail for the picture. It is not necessary to remove it to adjust the points gap.

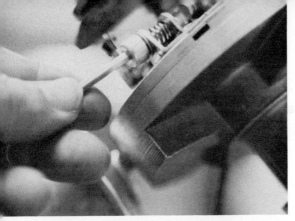

The window-type distributor can be adjusted by simply raising the metal window and inserting an Allen wrench inside. The top photo has the plastic cap removed to show what happens when the Allen wrench is inserted. It contacts a screw. When this spring-loaded screw is turned, it changes the contact points gap. Some tune-up kits for this type of distributor include a proper-size Allen wrench along with the contact points set, a condenser, and a new rotor.

attach the points. If this screw, which is eccentric (off center), is turned with a screwdriver, it will change the points gap in exactly the same way twisting the screwdriver blade in the slots does on the other type.

Window Type Adjustments

On the window-type distributors used by GM and some American Motors cars, the points can be adjusted without removing the cap from the distributor. They can also be adjusted while the engine is running, something you can't do with the other kinds.

The accompanying illustration shows how this is done. The metal window on the cap is raised and a hex wrench (Allen wrench) is inserted into a hex slot on a screw inside the window. The second half of the illustration has the cover removed so you can see what is happening when you insert the hex wrench. Turning the screw changes the setting of the points.

If you use a feeler gauge to determine the correct width of the gap, you have to take the cover off as you do with the other distributors. This procedure can be avoided, however. Here is the method some mechanics recommend:

1. Screw the adjustment clockwise until the engine falters. Do not go so far that you kill the engine.
2. Back off after the engine stutters *one full turn.*
3. Then twist the adjustment back in a half turn. You'll be close enough to the correct setting to get by.

Using the Dwell Meter

The only way you can get an exact setting on used points is by using a dwell meter. Whereas the feeler-gauge method of setting points measures the opening of the gap, the dwell meter measures the time the points are closed. Gap and dwell are tied together. The smaller the gap the greater the dwell. The smaller the dwell the bigger the gap.

Dwell is also known as "cam angle," and on some specs charts you may find it listed as such.

Dwell meters come in all sizes from big square boxes to small gadgets held in the hand. They all work alike. The meter has two connections. One (generally colored red to make determination easy) is clamped onto the connection on the *distributor side* of the coil. The other connection is the ground. This type of connection is for cars with *negative* ground. If your car has a positive ground, then the leads must be reversed. To find out which ground you have, check the battery. If the negative terminal is grounded, then you have a negative ground. Most cars have negative ground.

Once the connection is made, check the dwell meter dial with the engine. A needle moving across the dial will show you the degree of dwell. Take the reading while the engine is running at idle. If it agrees with the engine specifications, you are home free. If not, adjust the gap until it does.

On the window (external adjustment) type of distributor you have only to insert the Allen wrench and gently adjust until the dial reads the correct dwell. Your points are then properly adjusted.

Adjusting Dwell on Conventional Distributors

On conventional distributors things are a bit more complicated when you use a dwell meter. The hook-up is the same. Connect the red lead to the distributor side of the coil and the other to the ground (if you have a negatively grounded car).

Now since we must remove the distributor cap to see the points and adjust them, we will not be able to start the engine as we did with the window-type distributor. You can, of course, hook up the dwell meter, start the engine with the distributor cap in place, and get a dwell reading. But then you have to stop the engine, remove the cap, make a blind adjustment, replace the cap, and take another dwell reading. Heaven only knows how many times you'll have to do this before you get it on the mark.

So what we'll do is use the starter to turn the engine over. First, remove the coil wire from the center terminal tower of the distributor cap. Use a jumper wire to ground the coil wire to the engine or body frame. This is done so that the high-tension jolt of juice that is formed by the collapsing magnetic field in the coil will have a place to go.

Next remove the distributor cap. It is not necessary to remove any of the sparkplug wires. Just remove the cap and lay it to one side. You will not be able to hold the dwell meter, since you'll need one hand to operate the remote starter switch and the other to adjust the points. The remote starter switch (which will cost you about $2) is connected to the starter solenoid and permits you to start the engine from under the hood. If you don't have one, or your car is of the type that makes it difficult to hook a remote starter to it, you'll have to get someone to sit in the front seat and actuate the starter when you call out. Since the cap is off the distributor and the high-tension coil wire is grounded, the engine will not start, although it will grind away at cranking speed. Take your dwell reading and make your adjustments as quickly as possible. (*Caution:* you can very quickly run your battery down in this operation, for a starter pulls a very heavy charge of juice directly from the battery.)

After the correct adjustment is made, replace the distributor cap, unground the high-tension coil wire and put it back in place in the center tower of the distributor cap. Now start the engine and recheck the dwell at idle speed. You may find that there is a difference between the dwell at cranking speed and the dwell at idle speed. In this case you go back and do it over again, increasing or diminishing the dwell as the need may be.

Dwell Variation Test

A difference in dwell between the cranking speed and the idle speed can be expected. However, there should not be much variation in dwell between the idle speed and higher running speeds. The specs give the amount of tolerable variation. Generally there should not be more than 3 or 4 degrees.

To check for dwell variation you first disconnect the vacuum advance. This is the dashpot you see on the side of your distributor to which a line, generally rubber but occasionally of metal, runs to the carburetor. At certain speeds there is suction through this line which pulls a diaphragm that moves an arm. This arm is attached to the distributor breaker plate and advances the car's ignition timing at higher speeds.

We do not want any change in timing while we check dwell variation. So we remove the hose from the vacuum advance unit and plug the open end of this hose so that extra air will not be sucked into the carburetor during our tests.

Now with the engine running at idle speed, we check the dwell reading. Then increase the engine speed to 2,000 rpm (revolutions per minute) and note the new reading. It should be within the manufacturers' recommended reading—generally 3 or 4 degrees. If it does not, then you have trouble in the distributor. Its repair goes beyond simple tune-up.

Checking Rpm

There was a time when mechanics could judge the speed of an engine by ear. Some can still do pretty well on engines they are familiar with, but most of us can't. Modern engines are too quiet, for one thing. And the present emphasis on smog control makes it necessary to control our idle speeds more carefully than in the past. So the only real way to know that you are making your dwell variation test at 2,000 rpm is to check. This is done with a tachometer.

Many dwell meters, even the inexpensive ones, come with a tachometer circuit built in, and are tach/dwell or dwell/tach meters rather than purely dwell meters. To check the engine's rpm all you have to do is change the position of the switch, moving it from dwell to tach. One of the scales on the dial can then be read in rpm. You then adjust your throttle until you read 2,000 or whatever rpm you seek. Then slide the switch back to dwell and take a dwell reading.

One word of caution, however. During this check your engine must be not cold but at normal operating temperature; the choke on the carburetor must be in full open position. A cold engine is set to idle faster so that it won't die so easily before it warms up. If you check the rpm when the engine is cold, they will drop too low when the fast idle cam kicks out as the engine heats up.

Points Testing

Many tach/dwell meters also have a circuit to test the points. Again you merely shift the switch to the points position. If the needle jumps off the scale, indicating that no electricity at all is getting through, your points are open. The rubbing block is sitting on top of the cam lobe or close to it. Just tap your starter button enough to move it off and you'll begin to get a proper reading. Most of these points testers are weak voltmeters that test the voltage flowing through the points. They are usually set up to read in a "good" or "bad" section, so there is no complicated figuring to do. They are a great help in letting you know when your points need changing.

Double-Contact Distributors

In the ordinary run of stock cars you won't find many distributors with two sets of contact points in them, but they do occur. In this case you will have a four-lobe cam for an eight-cylinder car instead of the standard eight-lobe. There will be two sets of contact points, each connected to a separate coil. One set of points and one coil furnish the spark for four cylinders. The others are for the remaining four. These have to be synchronized according to the manufacturer's instructions.

Summary

The standard procedure for gapping points on a conventional distributor is as follows:

- Engine not running. Remove cap from distributor. Do not remove distributor wires.
- Place the rubbing block of the contact points set on the tip of the cam lobe. This can be done by lightly bumping the starter button—either from the switch inside the car or with a remote starter switch—until the rubbing block is on top of the cam. This takes a delicate touch and is some-

times hard for a beginner. If you have trouble, try this: remove the sparkplugs. This will eliminate compression, since the compressed gas will come out the plug holes. Then without compression the engine will turn over easily and you can move it into position by pulling on the fan belt. Also, there are available ring sets that slip over the cam and give you the proper lift on the rubbing block without going to the bother of setting the rubbing block on the cam's lobe. J. C. Whitney, the mail order people, have one for about $6.

- The top lobe of the cam, pressing against the rubbing block, will open the contact points to their widest gap. Measure this gap with a feeler gauge—if you are putting in new points.
- Check spec sheet for proper-size gap.
- Loosen the lock screw.
- Adjust the gap by turning the screwdriver blade in the adjusting slots or by turning the adjusting cam screw if no slots are provided. Adjust until the contact points fit snugly, but not tightly, against the flat surfaces of the feeler gauge.
- Tighten the lock screw and replace the distributor cap.

The procedure for adjusting the contact points on the window type distributor is as follows.

- With the engine running at idle speed, raise the window on the side of the distributor cap.
- Insert hex wrench in the adjusting screw inside the window. Use dwell meter to adjust according to specifications. If no dwell meter is available, turn adjusting screw clockwise until engine begins to falter. Then turn in the opposite direction one full turn, then screw in a half-turn. This gives an approximate setting only.

Directions for using the dwell meter:

- Connect the red lead of the dwell meter to the distributor side of the coil. Clip it over the terminal with the wire to the distributor in place. Connect the second lead wire to a good ground.
- If you have a window-type distributor, start the engine and read the dwell at idle speed.
- On conventional distributors, use a remote starter switch or have someone actuate the starter from the dashboard to turn over the engine at cranking speed. First, however, remove the coil wire, ground it with a jumper wire, and remove the distributor cap.
- Read the dwell meter at cranking speed, adjusting the contact-points gap to correct the dwell as the engine is turning.
- Replace the distributor cap and coil wire, leaving the dwell meter connected. Start the engine and read the dwell at idle speed. Idle dwell may be different from the dwell at cranking speed. So you may need to readjust, repeating the process until you get the manufacturer's spec.

Caution: Do not crank with the starter any longer than absolutely necessary. Starters pull heavy jolts of juice and you can very quickly run down your battery. Also, remove the vacuum advance hose and plug it before setting the dwell.

Chapter 8

ELECTRONIC IGNITION SYSTEMS

Setting and adjusting points has been a tune-up specialists' job since the first multicylinder engine was built for an automobile. In every breaker-point ignition system there is a slight change in ignition timing as the breaker points burn and the rubbing block wears. This causes the contact gap between the contacts to get gradually smaller. The dwell therefore gets bigger as the gap gets smaller. The only way to take care of this and keep correct timing has been to readjust or replace contact points sets at regular tuneup intervals.

Today we are moving into something entirely new—something that can eventually make changing points obsolete, will do away with ignition failures due to condenser failures, and will virtually eliminate the distributor as a primary concern in engine tune-up. The marvel that will do all this for us is the electronic ignition system.

The electronic ignition is not new. It has been around on an experimental status for a decade or so. In 1972 Chrysler made it standard equipment on its eight-cylinder cars sold in California, and optional on cars sold elsewhere. Then in 1973 General Motors announced that electronic ignition systems will be standard on GM cars in 1975, with installations on some models coming earlier.

89

This change will not immediately make replacing points obsolete. Older cars will be on the road for a long time to come. The average life of a car is ten years, but you'll find a lot of them still chugging long past this time. It will be at least 1985 or later before you can throw away your gap-setting feeler gauge and your dwell meter—unless of course you can afford to go buy a new car immediately.

How Electronic Ignition Works

In the electronic ignition system you still use the familiar coil, distributor advance systems, rotor and cap, wiring and sparkplugs. You do not have the cam, points, and condenser that you have in the conventional distributor, but you add a control unit and a dual ballast resistor.

The distributor will look the same (see accompanying photograph) except that the familiar lobed cam turning on the distributor shaft has been replaced with a "reluctor." The reluctor has one tooth for each cylinder. Since this distributor was made for the eight-cylinder Chrysler, it has eight teeth. Placed beside the reluctor, but *not* touching it, is a pickup unit. The pickup unit is a permanent magnet and a coil wound around a pole piece. There is a weak magnetic field in the pickup unit.

As the tooth of the gearlike reluctor passes the pickup unit, it increases the strength of the weak magnetic field. This increase in field strength at the pickup coil induces a *positive* voltage at one of the coil terminals. When the reluctor passes the air gap of the pickup unit, the strength of the magnetic field changes again, and a *negative* voltage is induced.

The voltage induced by the movement of the reluctor passing the pickup unit is very small. It is used as a *signal* to the control unit. This tiny signal triggers the electronic circuitry in the control unit, causing it to break the primary circuit from the coil. You will remember that in a regular distributor the circuit is broken by opening the points. Also in the regular distributor the condenser works with the points to speed up the collapse of the magnetic field and to reduce arcing, which burns the points. Since we have no points, the condenser is no longer needed.

What happens is that the battery current flows through the coil's primary circuit, building up a strong magnetic field, and thence into the control unit where it grounds back to the battery.

When the control unit receives its triggering burst of electricity from the pickup unit (caused by the reluctor passing the pickup unit in the distributor), this signal causes the control unit to cut off the primary circuit. This collapses the magnetic field in the coil just as opening the points does in a conventional distributor. The collapse induces in the secondary circuit a high tension current, which the distributor sends out to each individual spark plug.

Maintenance of the Electronic Ignition System

There are no normal periodic tune-up requirements for electronic ignition systems. The reluctor does not contact the pickup unit in the distributor, so there is no wear. There must be a .008-inch air gap between the two, but this is set upon installation and should not change with operation.

Dwell is determined by the control unit and will always be correct unless the unit is damaged. Because the control unit is sealed and has no moving parts, the dwell cannot be changed or adjusted.

The electronic system does not eliminate tune-up work, but it greatly simplifies tune-up by eliminating the need to check, regap and replace points and replace condensers.

In tuning a car with electronic ignition you follow the usual procedure in checking the battery, wiring, and all connections for tightness. Check your coil and the connections to and from the control unit. The round button on the control unit is the switching transistor. *Never touch it when the ignition is on. It packs quite a jolt.*

In the distributor, look to see that it is clean. Dirt, grease, and oil can work in if the cap doesn't fit tightly. Check the cap the same way you would for the regular systems, for the cap hasn't changed. The current will still flow in through the high-tension wire in the central tower and be distributed through each of the sparkplug wires to the plugs. Check the terminals in the cap for corrosion, and look for cracks in the insulation and for carbon tracks that indicate a short circuit. Change the rotor if it is pitted on the connections.

The new Chrysler electronic distributor has a "reluctor" A in place of the conventional cam and rubbing block. There is one tooth on the reluctor for each cylinder. As each tooth passes the pickup unit B a weak positive current is induced. This small charge acts as a "signal" to a control unit that turns the current in the coil on and off to collapse the electromagnetic field created by current flowing through the primary circuit. This is exactly what opening the points does in a conventional distributor. However, the electronic system eliminates points and condenser, two sources of tune-up trouble. C is the permanent magnet.

Electronic Ignition Repair

Electronic circuits can go bad just like anything else. Repair is not a part of tune-up. Checking out the electronic ignition system requires special test units. Chrysler has built an electronic ignition tester for use by service stations. Even if the price were low enough for the Sunday home mechanic to afford, he would need it so seldom that it wouldn't be worth buying. It is quite possible that as soon as electronic ignition systems become common you'll see inexpensive testing units on sale just as you now have inexpensive dwell meters.

As we mentioned earlier, the dwell meter does not go with the new electronic systems. However, the tachometer does. So if you buy a car with an electronic ignition and you have a dwell/tach meter, don't throw it away. The tachometer is essential for setting your carburetor.

The information given here is related to the Chrysler system. General Motors, according to a statement made by the company president to a congressional committee, will incorporate

The new electronic ignition system consists of a control unit A, the reluctor and pickup unit in the distributor B, and a dual ballast resistor unit C.

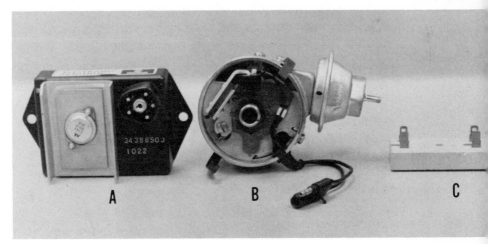

an electronic distributor, a new type of carburetor, and a catalytic muffler. The details of this system, set to be incorporated
on some 1974 and all 1975 GM cars, have not be revealed at
the time this was written.

The Dual Ballast Resistor

There is one other difference between the Chrysler system
and the conventional ignition. This is in the ballast resistor. The
ballast resistor gives so little trouble that most car owners don't
even know they have one.

They came about when cars switched to 12-volt systems.
The ballast resistor regulates the primary current throughout
the speed range of the car. At low speeds the ballast resistor
heats up and increases resistance, thus limiting the flow of the
primary current. At high speeds the resistor cools and allows
more current to flow. The resistor is made of a material that
increases resistance as it heats up.

A decrease in current is not desired for the cranking system
and there is a bypass, so that when you turn on the starter
switch the battery current does not flow through the ballast
resistor but goes full-voltage to the starter.

The ballast resistor in the Chrysler electronic ignition system
has a dual role. One section has a half-ohm ballast resistor just
like the one found on cars with breaker-point systems. It does
the same job. It maintains constant primary current as engine
speeds vary and it protects your coil against high current flow
at low engine speeds. The second section of the electronic
systems ballast resistor is a 5-ohm resistor. It protects the control unit by limiting current flow in the electronic circuit.

Can You Replace Your Distributor with an Electronic One?

Why not? It's too early to tell if the GM models will be
interchangeable, but the Chrysler ones are interchangeable

with other eight-cylinder distributors for their cars. You pull out your old distributor, put in the new one and wire in the control unit and new dual ballast resistor.

Because of the cost, this is probably practical only if your old distributor is so badly worn that it has to be replaced.

Chapter 9

TIMING

Up to this point we have followed the electrical current from the battery through the coil and the primary circuit, where it is controlled by the breaker points or—in the case of the new electronic distributors—by the reluctors and the control unit. This switching on and off of the primary circuit permits build-up and collapse of an electromagnetic field in the coil, thereby inducing high-tension current in the secondary circuit and providing the spark to fire the gas in our cylinders.

All this work to increase voltage will be useless if we cannot deliver the resulting spark to the sparkplug at precisely the exact split second. Getting the spark to fire at just the right moment is the job of *timing*.

Changing the dwell one degree will change the timing one degree, so we always set the dwell before we set the timing. When we speak of timing in automobile tune-up work we refer to *ignition timing*. (There is also something called valve timing, and certain gears must be correctly timed in assembly, but we will not concern ourselves with these cases.)

We must now go back to our original discussion on how an internal combustion engine works. We spoke of a four-cycle engine having an intake, compression, power, and exhaust

96

strokes. In timing we are concerned primarily with the compression stroke. This is when the rising piston squeezes the air/gas mixture in the cylinder into the small area of the combustion chamber in the cylinder head. The more this gas is compressed, the greater will be the force of its expanding gasses when it is burned. This is the basis of high-compression engines.

Fire in the Hole

The gas in the cylinder is fired by a spark jumping across the electrodes of the sparkplug. The fuel burns so rapidly that it seems to do so instantaneously, but this is not so. The fire starts just like a picnic bonfire. You hold a lighted match to the wood. It begins as a small blaze that spreads until it engulfs the entire pile.

The same process takes place in an automobile cylinder. The fire begins as a spark between the electrodes. This ignites the fuel between the electrodes of the plug. The initially small fire then spreads evenly through all the fuel in the combustion chamber.

Pointing this out may seem like a lot of unnecessary detail, but it is important in understanding why we have to time an engine so exactly. You will recall that when the piston moves as high as it will go in a cylinder it is at Top Dead Center. We want the full pressure of our burning fuel to push against the top of the piston at TDC or slightly thereafter. If the spark fires the gas too far before TDC, then the pressure of the burning gases is trying to force the piston down at the same time that the crankshaft is trying to force it up. You can see the trouble this would create. The piston can't go up and down at the same instant. So when the spark fires too early, the best that can happen is that you'll get a power-robbing preignition knock or "ping." At worst, you'll hammer a hole in your piston, which will nick your wallet for an expensive repair job.

On the other hand, if the spark fires too late—too long after the piston reaches TDC—and starts down again, you lose compression because the fuel is not so tightly packed. This robs us of power also.

Engine Timing

Our job, therefore, in engine timing is to insure that the "fire" starts in the cylinder just far enough ahead of TDC that it will build up and exert its full force on the piston at Top Dead Center or slightly thereafter.

As we mentioned in talking about dwell, a circle is measured in degrees. The flywheel on the end of the crankshaft is a circle. When the flywheel makes one full turn it moves 360 degrees. If it turns only halfway around, it turns 180 degrees. What we need to know is how many degrees before Top Dead Center we want to start the fire in our cylinder so that it will blaze up to full force when the piston gets to the top.

You get the number of degrees from your spec sheet. It varies with different automobile designs and with engine rpm. Here are a few examples:

> 1972 American Motors, all engines are 5 degrees at 500 rpm except the 258 cu in. 6-cylinder (1-bbl), which is 3 degrees.
> Chevrolet 1972 400 cu in. V-8 (4-bbl) is 8 degrees at 600 rpm.
> 1972 Dodge 360 cu in. V-8 (2-bbl) is TDC at 700 rpm.
> 1972 Plymouth 198 cu in. 6-Cylinder (1-bbl) is 2.5 degrees at 800 rpm.

In order to meet smog requirements, manufacturers have been been changing engine timing and rpm specs. Idle speeds on newer cars are running somewhat higher than on older models. Since so much smog-emission work is still experimental, you may find timing and rpm specs changing still more as time goes by. All you can do is check the latest spec sheets.

Timing

The timing mark on this 1969 Chevy V-8 is engraved on the balancer just behind the fan belt on the driver's side of the engine. The pointer scale opposite the timing mark shows how many degrees the number one spark plug is firing before or after TDC when the marks are illuminated by a strobe timing light. Since each mark on this particular model is for two degrees, in this picture the timing mark shows that the engine is firing four degrees before Top Dead Center.

Timing Marks

In order to permit you to determine the number of degrees your ignition system is firing before TDC, the car makers have provided timing marks. At one time these timing marks were cut on the surface of the flywheel. There was a tiny window in the flywheel housing so you could see them. You won't find them there any more except on older cars. Today timing marks are found on the vibration dampener or on the fan-belt pulley.

The accompanying photo shows the timing markings on a 1968 Chevrolet engine. We are looking at the left side of the engine as determined from the driver's side. What we see is the bottom of the fan belt and the fan-belt pulley. *A* is the fan belt, *B* the fan-belt pulley, *C* the vibration dampener, a heavy wheel to smooth out vibration, *D* the shaft from the crankshaft that runs the fan-belt pulley, *E* the timing scale. Notice that the scale has a number of black lines and the letters *A-O-R*. *A* on the scale means advance, *R* means retard, and *O* is Top Dead Center.

Opposite the lines of the scale you will see a black line on the vibration dampener wheel. This is the engine timing mark. Each of the numerous marks on the scale itself stand for two degrees each *on this particular engine.*

The Timing Light

The timing mark on the dampener spins, of course, when the engine is running. We make it "stand still" with a timing light —which is actually a strobe light that fires in time with the Number 1 sparkplug. Since this light fires each time the mark on the wheel spins past the scale, the timing mark appears to stand still during the split second it is illuminated by the strobe light. Therefore, it will appear to be stopped opposite the scale. You read the position. In this photograph, the timing light would show that we are timed at four degrees before top dead center.

Since this is a 1968 302-cu in. small Chevvy engine, we check the spec sheet and see that we are right on the money at an idle speed of 900 rpm.

You use a tachometer or your tach/dwell meter to determine the rpm before you check your timing with the timing light. If the rpm is not according to spec, adjust the fast idle screw on your carburetor according to direction given in the carburetor section of this book.

Adjusting Timing

Suppose your timing is incorrect—and most of the time it always seems to be—then what? Then do this:
- Disconnect the vacuum hose from the vacuum advance on the side of the distributor. We are setting *initial timing* at idle speed and don't want any danger of the vacuum advance increasing our timing. Plug the vacuum hose to keep it from sucking air into the carburetor.
- Check the rpm of the engine and set to manufacturer's

specifications for initial timing. Use a tach meter to determine the rpm.

- Timing is changed by rotating the distributor. This is done
  by loosening the hold-down bracket on the block that
  keeps the distributor in place. The bracket is secured by a
  bolt. The bracket is loosened just enough for you to turn
  the distributor in either direction.

- The illustration shows the hold-down bracket bolt on a
  small Ford V-8 engine. This picture was made of an engine
  that had been removed from a car. Sunk in an engine well
  of a car, the hold-down bracket is not so easily seen on
  many cars. You have to feel for it, running your hand under
  the distributor. Also, the space is often so narrow that you
  can't get an ordinary wrench in to loosen the bolt on some
  model cars. In such cases, you must use an offset wrench,
  which is a wrench with a crooked handle. You can buy
  one to twist around your distributor if you must. You can't
  use just *any* offset wrench; you must have one to fit your
  particular model of car. To use the wrench, you slip it over
  the hold-down bolt by feel and twist just enough so that

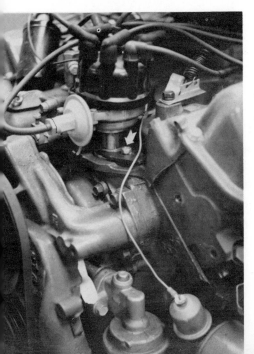

*This shows the hold-down bracket
and bolt on a small Ford V-8 engine.
This bolt must be loosened to adjust
the timing.*

you can grasp the side of the distributor and turn it fairly easy in either direction.

- Connect the timing light according to the manufacturer's directions. This will depend upon the type of light you use. The cheaper neon-type lights (available for about $2.50 up) are connected to the Number 1 plug. They work, but are very weak. This means that they are impossible to see in bright light—you have to shade them or work in a darkened garage. (Be sure the garage has enough ventilation to prevent carbon monoxide poisoning.) You must be very careful that you don't let your hand contact the moving fan while checking the timing with these weak lights. Occasionally backyard mechanics try to get the light up close, to make make up for the lack of brightness, and lose a finger in the process. A better light is the power timing light. It is connected to the car's battery for power and has another wire to the Number 1 sparkplug to trigger the flash. It gives a brilliant white light. Another type of power light connects to a regular a-c light current with one wire running to the car's Number 1 plug to trigger the flash at the right time. It has the advantage of not putting a drain on your car battery, but also the disadvantage of having to be near a house current receptacle to be used. Power timing lights are much more expensive.

- Point the timing light at the timing marks on the vibration dampener. These may be on the right or left side of the car, depending upon the make. The light will fire each time the Number 1 sparkplug fires. On in-line American engines (that is, engines that have the cylinders in one straight line), the Number 1 cylinder is always the first cylinder, counting the one nearest the radiator as the front. On V-8 engines the Number 1 cylinder is also in the front of the engine, but it may be either the right or left of the two front cylinders. On American Motors V-8 engines the Number

1 cylinders are on the left as viewed from the driver's seat. General Motors cars also have their Number 1 cylinders on the front left, except Cadillac, which has its Number 1 cylinder on the right front. Chrysler is on the left, but Ford is on the right. Remember, this direction is from the driver's position. If you are looking at the engine across the radiator, the direction is just the opposite.

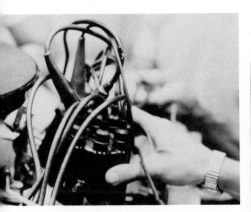

A Sun timing light is shown in use here. The light is pointed down between the radiator and the engine to check the timing.

Once the hold-down bracket bolt is loosened, timing is accomplished by slightly rotating the distributor while observing the timing marks on the vibration or dynamic balancer back of the fan belt pulley. This is done while the engine is idling.

Turning the Distributor

- If the timing mark does not line up with the proper mark on the timing scale, then you slowly rotate the distributor as shown in the accompanying photograph. Which direction you turn—whether right or left—depends upon whether you want to advance or retard the spark, and also on whether your distributor rotates clockwise or counterclockwise.
- Spec sheets usually tell you if you have a counterclockwise or a clockwise rotating distributor. If you can't tell any other way, remove the distributor cap and either touch the remote starter switch or have someone turn the engine

over from the dashboard starter switch. Then you can see which way it turns. Some distributors have a small arrow on the rotor to indicate the direction. Once you determine the direction the distributor rotor turns, follow these rules:

- If you need to *retard* the spark to bring it up to specs, rotate the body of the distributor *in the direction the rotor turns.*
- If you want to *advance* the spark, rotate the distributor in the *opposite* direction from the way the rotor turns.
- When the marks are lined up according to specs, then you tighten down the holddown bolt, and that's it.

Static Timing

By using a test light it is possible to time a car without a timing light. A test light is nothing more than two leads attached to a small bulb. You can buy them in any auto parts store.

Static timing is done with the engine dead. Attach one lead of the test light to the distributor side of the coil and the other to the ground. Tap the starter to move the engine a little at a time until you line up the timing marks according to specs. In other words, if the timing is supposed to be four degrees before TDC, line them up that way. If you can't tap the starter button gently enough to move the marks into position, try removing the sparkplugs and pulling the fan belt to move the engine until the timing marks line up to specifications.

We have lined up the timing marks according the way they should be when the Number 1 plug fires, but we have not changed the timing. This can be done only by rotating the distributor. Before, when we timed the car with a timing light, we had the engine running. With the strobe light on the timing light, we rotated the distributor until the marks lined up correctly when the Number 1 plug fired.

In static timing, with the engine not running, we work backward from this. We start by lining up the timing marks the way they should be when the number one plug fires. Then we change the distributor so that the number one plug fires at the right time.

How do we know how much to turn the distributor? That's where our test light comes in. We connect it to the distributor side of the coil and to the ground. Now we turn on the car's ignition switch but do *not* actuate the starter. This permits electricity to flow through the coil and the primary circuit to the points and into the ground. The test light bulb will not burn as long as the points are closed. This is because electricity follows the path of least resistance. The bulb offers resistance. So the electricity takes the easier way through the points.

But the instant the points open, the electricity, having no other place to go, turns through the test-light circuit and the bulb burns. If you set the timing mark according to specs and the light does not glow, you are out of time. You loosen the distributor hold-down bolt and turn the distributor until the light just comes on. Your ignition is then in time.

How accurate static timing is depends upon how accurately you can determine the exact instant the light bulb glows. You should be able to set timing in this manner close enough to get by. In fact, some foreign-car manuals recommend static timing.

The test light described here is nothing more than a continuity tester, but for less than $2 you can buy a battery-powered test light. It furnishes its own power so you don't have to turn on the car ignition to test a circuit. They come with instructions telling you how to use them for static timing.

Vacuum and Mechanical Advances

The timing necessary to get the best operation from a car at idle speed is not the same as the timing the car must have speeding along at 65 miles per hour. The timing we set so carefully with our timing light is the *initial timing*. Initial, in this case, means the "starting point."

Why do you need to advance the timing as a car goes faster? O.K., we have determined, in talking about initial timing, that the fuel in our cylinders does not burn instantaneously. It has to start and build up to a roaring flame, just as a bonfire is set. Therefore we time the spark to start the fire sufficiently before Top Dead Center so that we get the full force of the burning when we need it to push the piston down. In the average car design this initial advance timing runs from three to six and sometimes eight degrees before TDC, *at idle speed.* Now when we speed up the engine, it is going to take just as long for the fire to build up, but the engine—jumping from a previous 500 rpm to 2,000, 3,000 or maybe 5,000 rpm—moves up to ten times as fast. Therefore we have to "light the fire" earlier to keep the fast-running engine from getting to TDC and starting down before the fire builds up.

This necessary advance is taken care of automatically by the distributor's vacuum advance and centrifugal advance—two separate mechanisms.

The Vacuum Advance

The vacuum advance unit is the metal dashpot arrangement on the side of the distributor. Inside is a spring-loaded diaphragm that is pulled by vacuum from the carburetor. A link arm is connected to the diaphragm and to the breaker plate inside the distributor. As the diaphragm is sucked in by the vacuum, it changes the position of the breaker plate and advances the timing.

This vacuum advance is in addition to the automatic advance of the centrifugal advance system. The vacuum advance, which is an important feature in fuel economy, has been under severe attack in recent years as a pollutant. Laws have been advocated to remove them from cars. However, tests tend to prove that disconnecting the vacuum advance increases the danger of valves' becoming damaged from overheating.

The vacuum advance A is mounted on the side of the distributor. The vacuum hose B leads to the carburetor.

This is the top-mounted centrifugal advance system on GM window-type external adjustment distributors. The speed of the revolving distributor shaft causes the weights A and B to swing out. This moves the breaker plate mounted below and advances the timing.

Here the breaker plate has been removed to show the centrifugal advance mechanism mounted inside the distributor. As the shaft spins, weights A and B are moved outward by centrifugal force. This moves the breaker plate and advances the timing. The two pins in the two slots limit the outward movement of the weights.

From a tune-up standpoint, about all you can do is see that there is no binding in the linkage of the vacuum advance and that the diaphragm is working. You can suck on the hose and hear the diaphragm move against the spring. Check out the hose and its connection at the distributor and at the engine manifold for leaks.

The Centrifugal Advance

The centrifugal advance consists of spring-loaded weights. As the distributor shaft revolves faster with increased speed, these weights work against their springs and fly outward under push of centrifugal force. Centrifugal force is the same thing that makes a car lean outward when it swings around a curve. The movement of these weights, which varies with the speed of the engine, changes the position of the breaker plate in the distributor and advances the timing.

In the conventional distributor, the centrifugal advance weights are located under the breaker plate. In the window type of distributor, they are located above the points. In both cases, despite the different positions, they operate on the same principle.

About all that can be done on basic tune-up is to check the weights for free outward movement to insure that they are not binding. If you suspect that the springs are weak and need replacing, the most you can do is remove the distributor and get it checked out on a distributor tester, which will show the degree of advance at all speeds. Distributor testers run into the thousands of dollars and are not something you can pick up for your backyard work. If you get preignition knocking or loss of power at increased speeds, you might suspect the advance systems. Other conditions can cause similar symptoms, and the advance is just one thing to check out. Very rarely do you hear of anybody complaining about the advance systems.

Chapter 10

SPARKPLUGS

Continuing to trace the path of the battery current, after it is "distributed" by the distributor, the high-tension current generated by the coil goes along the sparkplug wires to the sparkplug.

The sparkplug is the whole reason for all that came before. The battery, the coil, the primary circuit, the points, the secondary circuit, and the distributor rotor are all there for the single purpose of getting fire across the electrodes of the sparkplug.

The main parts of a sparkplug are

- *The terminal*—to which the secondary high-tension wire from the distributor is attached.
- *The insulator*—the white ceramic material that comprises the upper part of the sparkplug. It also consists of a continuing section that extends under . . .
- *The shell*—the metal section in the center of the plug, which has flattened areas for the sparkplug wrench to grasp.
- Below the shell are the threads that screw the plug into the block.
- *The center electrode* extends from the nose of the insulator straight down out of the bottom of the plug.
- The *side electrode* curves under the center electrode.

109

Operation of a Sparkplug

The high-tension surge of current comes through the sparkplug wire, travels straight through the center electrode, and jumps the gap between the center electrode and the side electrode. The current then passes through the side electrode and grounds into the block by going through the shell threads. As the spark jumps the gap, it ignites the fuel mixture in the cylinder.

The terminals of a sparkplug take a tremendous punishment. They extend down into the combustion chamber. They are burned by temperatures ranging from ambient (same as the outside air) to as much as 4000°F. Then they are hammered by pressures ranging from normal air to as much as 600 pounds per square inch (psi) as the fuel is compressed around them and then expanded by burning. These high temperatures and pressures may build up as many as 40 times a second when the car is running at a high speed.

The parts of a sparkplug are A, terminal; B, manufacturer's code, C, insulator top; D, manufacturer's code repeated; E, metal shell; F, gasket; G, threads; H, center electrode; and I, side electrode.

Under these conditions it is not surprising that plugs fail early. Replacing them is one of the basic jobs of engine tune-up. It is a simple job of screwing out the old plug, setting the correct gap on the new plug, and screwing it back in place of the discard. However, the engine wells on some modern cars are so small and have so many accessories jammed under the hood—smog devices and air conditioners, among others—that it sometimes becomes a difficult job to get to your plugs. Back in the 1950s there was one model of an expensive car that cost about $50 in a service station just to change the plugs because the mechanics had to remove so much equipment before they could get to them.

Choosing the Right Plug

Manufacturers either stamp on the metal shell, print on the porcelain top insulator, or put in both places a code number series that identifies the individual type of plug.

It is very important that you use the right plug. A plug that is too long may screw in so deeply that the rising piston will strike it. One that is too short may not extend into the combustion chamber enough to ignite the gas. Also, there is the matter of heat range, since there are "hot" and cold" plugs.

The terms "hot" and "cold" plugs refer to the ability of a plug to get rid of heat, passing it through the ceramic insulation to the shell and then to the water circulating through the water jacket in the block. Using a plug with the wrong heat range can mess up your ignition.

A plug that conducts heat away rapidly is a "cold" plug. One that that gets rid of the heat more slowly is a "hot" plug. You can tell the difference by the length of the shell. The longer the shell (and the ceramic insulation under it), the hotter the plug.

The manufacturer's code number has a letter or number in it that indicates the plug's heat range. Normally, you check your specs or use the number on your old plugs to order new ones. If the number on your old plugs does not agree with the specs, it does not necessarily mean that you've been running the wrong plugs. The specs give the plugs the car needed when it was new and are based on average driving. If the car is worn or is either driven too slowly (as in city delivery) or at constant top speeds, then it may have been necessary for the mechanic before you to go to a hotter or a colder plug. If your car has been giving good service with these numbered plugs, then stick with them.

Determining the Right Heat Range

You can determine if the heat range of your plugs is correct by checking the color of used plugs. If you have a plug with the proper heat range, the insulator will be light tan in color and will be clean. If you are running a plug that is too hot, the insulator may have a white appearance and the electrodes may be burned. If the plug is too cold, its electrodes will probably be fouled with carbon.

Under the best conditions the beating that plugs take wears them out. Plugs should be replaced every 10,000 miles, and you'll do well to take them out, clean them and reset the gap between the center electrode and the side electrode every 5,000 miles. Oxides, carbon, and deposits build up on the electrodes and insulator.

The only successful way to clean a plug is to sand blast it in a regular sparkplug cleaner. Digging the carbon out from between the insulator and the shell with a sharp-pointed instrument doesn't work well, and you could damage the insulator. Solvents work to some degree, but generally you are better off just replacing the plug if it is in bad shape. In a well-running car, with the right heat range of plug, at the 5,000- or 6,000-mile check you shouldn't have to do more than scrape off the electrodes and file them flat. Then you regap.

Gapping the Plugs

The gap between the electrodes of your sparkplugs is as important as the gap in your distributor. If the gap is too wide, the spark can't get across. If too narrow, it can burn your electrodes excessively or even fail to ignite the gas. It is necessary to refer to your spec sheets to get the correct gap. Just as examples, all American Motors engines for 1972 are gapped at .035; Buick is .040; Chevvy is .035 for all models; Chrysler is .035; Dodge is .030 for the 97.5 cu in., 4-cylinder engine and .035 for the others; Ford is .034 for all 1972 models except the 98 cu in., 4-cylinder, which is .030; Olds is .040 and Plymouth is .035 for all models except the 91.3 cu in., 4-cylinder, which is .025. These 1972 figures may vary in earlier and later models, and you should always check the specs before setting the plug gaps.

A round feeler gauge is used for gapping sparkplugs.

The gap between the electrodes should be checked with a wire gauge. If the two surfaces (of the center and side electrodes) are not exactly flat, then a flat feeler gauge will not give a true reading.

If the gap size is not up to specs, bend the *side* electrode to bring it to the proper size. It is extremely important to bend the side electrode and not the center. Bending the center electrode can crack or break the insulation ceramic, leading to shorts and misfires. Some gap gauges have a gapping tool built in for use in bending the side electrode.

Seating the Plugs

In replacing sparkplugs care must be taken to screw them in straight, so you will not get them jammed by cross-threading. This is a special danger of back plugs or those hidden under smog or air-conditioning devices, where you have to go by feel. On some cars it may be necessary to use offset wrenches or universal joints on your deep socket wrench to get to them.

We should also add here the precaution that you should clean dirt and grit from around your plug wells before removing plugs. This is to prevent foreign matter from falling into the cylinders. Most mechanics use a blast of compressed air to clean around the plugs before they take them out. An air compressor not being a common item in most home garages, you can blow around your plugs with an automobile tire pump. Some instructors recommend that you loosen your plugs enough so that compression from the engine will leak past the poor seat and blow any foreign matter away. I prefer to use the pump. It's faster and you don't have to go back and finish screwing out the plug.

You may encounter two different types of seats on sparkplugs. The ordinary one is a flat base with a round metal gasket that compresses when the plug is screwed down. The second type you'll find on Fords is called the "tapered seat." Instead of having a flat ring around the threads for the compressible gasket to press against, these plugs are machined at an angle that fits into a corresponding angle in the sparkplug hole. Tapered seat plugs do not require a gasket.

Torqueing the Plug

It is very important that sparkplugs be tightened properly. Mechanics call this "torqueing." If plugs are not screwed down tight enough, compression may leak out through the threads. Also, in the case of plugs employing gaskets, if the base of the plug does not squeeze tightly enough against the gasket it may interfere with the passage of heat and make the plugs run hotter than normal.

Another danger is that if you screw the plug in too tightly (overtorqueing) you can stretch the metal and change the

A torque wrench, which measures the pounds of pressure placed on bolts and spark plugs, is an extremely handy tool, for it insures that beginner mechanics will not strip threads by overtightening.

spark gap setting. In cars with aluminum heads, you can also strip the threads more easily than you might think.

Because of these dangers car makers generally specify the correct torque for their engines. As a general rule, specified torque for 14-mm plugs range from 20 to 25 pounds. (American Motors recommends 25–30 foot pounds.) Tapered seat plugs draw less torque than regular plugs, since you don't have a metal gasket to compress.

Torque (defined as a "twisting force") is measured in foot pounds with a wrench that has a built-in spring-loaded dial. This provides excellent insurance against the dangers of too much torque. Although it is not cheap, the torque wrench has other applications, of course, besides changing sparkplugs. It is one of the most valuable tools a mechanic can have.

But suppose you don't have a torque wrench and don't seem likely to be able to afford one. Then what? Well, some experienced mechanics can tell from the pressure they put on a wrench. If you lack their experience, try this: Tighten the plug in the hole until it fits snugly, then give a quarter-turn more. This is for gasket type plugs. Give only an eighth extra turn with tapered seat plugs.

Don't Oil the Plug Threads

For some reason or another beginners get the idea that they should oil the threads of sparkplugs to make them go in more easily. The trouble is that it makes them go in too easily. The result is danger of overtorqueing, since you'll have less friction between the plug threads and those in the block or head. Also, graphite, grease, or oil used to lubricate the threads may act as a barrier to keep heat from flowing readily from the plug to the block and, again, cause overheating of the block.

Get the Wires back Right

When you change sparkplugs you naturally have to remove the sparkplug wires. This is no problem. Remember to grasp the metal boot at the end of the wire and turn it to break the seal before pulling off gently by grasping the boot. Do not grab the wire and jerk, unless you already have a new wire to put in the place of the one you're trying to ruin.

The big problem for a beginner is not getting the wire off the the plug but getting it back on the right plug when you're done. Some strange things happen when sparkplug wires get mixed up. You can have your engine trying to run two ways at once or even completely backward.

The most positive way to insure that you get the wires back correctly is to take one off at a time, replace the plug and put the wire back on again before you go on to the next plug. If you need to remove all the wires at once for some reason, then put a piece of tape on each wire and write its number. Use these numbers as your reassembly guide.

This applies to marking the plug ends of the wires. If you also remove the wires from their towers in the distributor cap, you have another kind of problem—for the wires do not go into the distributor cap in the same order that they go on the plugs. If you remove the wires entirely, it will be necessary to mark which plug belongs to which tower.

Your Engine's Firing Order

Suppose you get them mixed up, or the numbers fall off, or you forget to number them, or you just want to wire your engine professionally. Then how do you figure out where the wires go?

In that case you have to know the "firing order" of your car, and the way the cylinders are numbered. Many later-model cars have the firing order molded on the block. Otherwise, you have to go to your specs.

In talking about timing earlier, we mentioned how to find the Number 1 cylinder of an engine. In an in-line engine the cylinders are numbered straight from the first cylinder. In a four-cylinder the numbers would be 1-2-3-4, with Number 1 being the front cylinder next to the radiator and Number 4 the back cylinder closest to the driver. The same system holds true for the six and straight eight (if you can find one these days).

The numbering of the V-8 engine is more complicated. The Number 1 cylinder is at the front, but it may be on the left or right side, depending upon the peculiarities of the manufacturer. Then in some cars the number alternates from one bank to the second bank. For example the numbering might be like this:

    Left bank viewed from in front of car   1-3-5-7
    Right bank viewed from in front of car 2-4-6-8
Or it might be like this:
    Left bank viewed from in front of car   2-4-6-8
    Right bank viewed from in front of car 1-3-5-7
Or it could be this way:
    Left bank viewed from in front of car   5-6-7-8
    Right bank viewed from in front of car 1-2-3-4

These numbers are the *cylinder numbers.* The *firing order* of these cylinders does not run 1-2-3-4 in order because you want to fire one in front and then one farther down the crankshaft, jumping around so that you get an even flow of pressure when the engine is running. How you jump around is called the *firing order.*

The rotor of a distributor travels around in a circle. When it touches the Number 1 wire position, the plug in the Number 1 cylinder will fire. Then the rotor moves to the second distributor position, but this does not necessarily fire the Number 2 cylinder. It fires the second cylinder in the *firing order,* which might happen to be Number 5, 6, or even 8 in the numbering.

Let's take an example of an in-line engine. We'll discuss the six-cylinder engines used for Buick, Chevvy, Olds, and Pontiac because General Motors uses the same numbering and firing order on engines for all these models.

Here are the cylinder numbers: 1-2-3-4-5-6
Here's the firing order: 1-5-3-6-2-4

When the engine is running, the Number 1 cylinder fires first, then the next click of the distributor rotor sends the spark to the next-to-last cylinder. Then come cylinders 3, 6, 2, and 4.

As an example of how the V-8 engine works, let's take a Ford. The cylinder numbers are (numbered from radiator end of engine):

1-2-3-4
5-6-7-8

The firing order is   1-3-7-2-6-5-4-8

Once you know the cylinder numbers and the firing order, all you need is the position of the Number 1 wire on the distributor. Actually your engine would run regardless of which distributor wire you chose to make Number 1—if there were sufficient room to turn the distributor to time it and to get it into place. If you choose the wrong Number 1 position and then got the rest of the wires in their correct order in relation to Number 1, you might not be able to change the timing because the vacuum advance on the side of the distributor would jam against the block.

In *many* cases the Number 1 wire is the one pointing directly toward the front of the car, but not every time. The best way is to mark the Number 1 wire before you take the wires off. You find it by determining the Number 1 cylinder according to your specs and tracing the wire to the distributor. Most spec sheets list the position of the Number 1 wire.

Putting the Wires in Place

You will notice, in rewiring your plugs, that the wires are of a different length. This is because the plugs closest to the distributor will be shorter and those farthest from the distributor will be longer. This seems too simple to even bother to mention, but you'd be surprised at the number of beginners who will use a long wire for the close plugs and then find that the shorter ones left won't reach from the distributor to the back plugs.

- To actually put the new wires in place, begin with the Number 1 terminal in the distributor. Press the wire's terminal firmly into the tower of the distributor cap and then push down the rubber boot that keeps dirt and grease from getting into the connection.
- Next take the opposite end of the wire and connect it to the sparkplug in the Number 1 cylinder. Press down firmly to insure contact and then pull the rubber boot down into position to protect the connection.
- How you proceed with the second wire depends upon whether the distributor rotor revolves clockwise or counterclockwise. The better spec sheets list distributor rotation direction in their charts. If you can't find the specs, remove the distributor cap and turn the engine over with the remote starter and see which way it turns.

  If the rotor revolves clockwise, then that is the way you put on the rest of the wires—in the same direction that the hands of a clock would move.

Follow the Firing Order

In the first tower we placed the Number 1 cylinder wire. In the adjacent tower *clockwise* of the Number 1 wire we put our next wire, but we refer to the firing order to see which plug we will connect it to. Going back to the examples we used earlier, we'll take the six-cylinder in-line GM engine, which has a firing order of 1-5-3-6-2-4.

So the second distributor wire will run to the Number 5 cylinder, as determined by the cylinder numbers: 1-2-3-4-5-6.

The third distributor wire goes to the Number 3 cylinder, and the fourth to the Number 6 cylinder, the fifth to the Number 2 cylinder and the sixth and last wire to the Number 4 cylinder.

You operate in a similar manner on four cylinder in-line engines and on V-8 engines.

Wiring should be checked at each tune-up and replaced if frayed, or if the insulation is cracked. You can use an ohmmeter to test resistance in the wire and replace the wire if it is excessive. A battery-powered test light hooked to each end of the wire will tell you if there is a break in the wire under the insulation.

Summary

- Sparkplugs must be kept clean and properly gapped and should be replaced every 10,000 miles.
- In replacing new plugs, check specs and get the proper plug for your car so you will have the correct "reach" and heat range.
- When plugs are replaced they should be torqued properly, because if they are tightened too much it can stretch the metal and change the gap clearances. Also if plugs are screwed into an aluminum head, there is greater danger of stripped threads. Use a torque wrench to be right.

- In gapping a plug, be sure to bend the *outside* electrode. Never bend the center electrode.
- The procedure for reinstalling spark plug wires is:
1. Determine cylinder numbers, firing order and position of the Number 1 wire on the distributor.
2. Determine the direction of rotor turn in the distributor, either clockwise or counterclockwise.
3. Place one end of the wires in the circle of towers around the distributor cap. The center tower is for the high-tension wire from the coil.
4. Attach the wire from the Number 1 tower of the distributor to the Number 1 cylinder plug.
5. Attach the second wire from the distributor (which would be clockwise in a clockwise rotating distributor) to the second plug in the *firing order,* and so on.

Chapter 11

THE FUEL SYSTEM

The electrical system ends with the electrodes of the spark-plugs. We have gotten the spark from the battery to the plugs for the purpose of setting fuel afire at precisely the right moment. Now we must insure that the fuel, in the right dilution and amount, is in the cylinders for the spark to ignite.

The fuel system begins with the gas tank. A line from the gas tank runs to a fuel pump that draws the gas up and pushes it through a filter to the carburetor. The fuel pump and lines do not require periodic maintenance and are not included in the usual service-station tune-up job, although they should be.

The filter can be removed and replaced. Older-type cars once had settling bowls in the line where water and heavier contaminants would settle below the lighter gasoline. You loosened the holding clips, removed the glass bowl, emptied and cleaned it and put it back on. Most cars today have the filter in the line, usually up close to the carburetor. The most popular type has an accordion-pleated filter element, which is not cleaned, but replaced.

The gasoline fuel, after it passes through the filter, goes to the carburetor—a most important element in the car.

123

How the Carburetor Works

The carburetor on a car works exactly like an atomizer on a woman's dressing table. When you put a liquid in the bottom and blow air across the top, a mist comes out. In fact, Charles Duryea, one of the brothers who developed the horseless carriage, used a perfume atomizer in their first engine before he developed the carburetor as we know it today.

Forgetting for the moment all the gadgets and extra circuits that are built into a carburetor, here is how a carburetor works.

The carburetor is a bowl into which the fuel pump forces gasoline. Riding in the bowl is a float that rises and falls with the level of gas in the bowl. This float is attached to a plug seated in the mouth of the gas line. When the bowl is full of gas, the float rises and the plug blocks the line so no more gas will enter the bowl. The gas level drops as the fuel is used by the car. The float goes down, opening the gas line so that more gas will flow in. This arrangement insures that there will always be a certain level of gas in the float bowl.

Adjoining the float bowl is an "air pipe." Outside air flows through an air cleaner into this pipe. The air coming in gets mixed with gas inside this pipe. The bottom end of the air pipe leads to the intake manifold, where it is stored until the engine's intake valves open. Then the gas and air mixture flows into the cylinders to be burned.

Air flows through the carburetor because the cylinder acts like an air pump. When the piston rises on the exhaust stroke, it pushes all the air out of the cylinder. Then when the piston descends on the intake stroke, the interior of the cylinder becomes a vacuum. When the intake valve opens, air rushes in. This process, because of lower pressure, pulls more air through the air horn of the carburetor.

Where the Gas Comes In

The pipe that permits air to flow through the air cleaner and into the intake manifold is not the same size all the way through. The center, in the area where it passes the gas float bowl, is more narrow than the rest of the pipe. This choked area is called a "venturi." A venturi in the carburetor acts the same as a nozzle on a hose.

What happens is that the air is being pulled through the pipe by the pumping action of the piston on the intake stroke. The air rushing into the pipe gets jammed at the venturi. This builds up pressure as the air tries to get through the smaller hole. Then the air going through the venturi, since it is escaping from the high-pressure choke-up above the venturi, loses pressure. It speeds up, spreading back out as it leaves the venturi and thus aiding in lowering the air pressure in the venturi.

The difference between the high pressure above the venturi and the lower pressure in and below the venturi is known as the "pressure drop."

This pressure drop is what creates the so-called "vacuum" in the carburetor.

Now if we put a small connecting tube from the gasoline float bowl to the venturi, we will have a means of drawing gas into the air stream. Since the air pressure in the float bowl is the same as the outside air, and since the air pressure in the venturi is lower, gas will be sucked out of the connecting tube into the air stream, where it will be vaporized and sucked into the intake manifold and then into the cylinder.

Air/Fuel Ratio

Gasoline will not burn unless it is mixed with the proper amount of air. The proper mixture at sea level is about 14 parts of air to 1 part of gasoline. If there is too much gasoline in the mixture, the air/fuel ratio is said to be too "rich." If there is too much air for the amount of gas, then the mixture is too "lean."

The amount of air and gasoline mixed together in the carburetor depends upon the size of the carburetor jets and the fuel mixture screws as well as upon the design of the carburetor. Ever since the big push on reducing car pollution many carburetors are coming with the fuel-mixture ports sealed, so there is nothing you can do about them. All new cars are equipped with limiter caps on the fuel mixture screws (where used) and on the idle-adjustment screws. Limiter caps limit the amounts of adjustment you can make and cannot be legally removed from a car.

Carb Variations

I once saw a class in automobile carburation make a list of the different kinds, models and variations of carburetors. They quit at a hundred and they probably didn't get half of them. All carburetors work on the same principle—that of air pumped by the piston through a venturi where it sucks gas from the float bowl and atomizes the gas, which is then drawn into the intake manifold.

But there the exact similarity ends. How they go about modifying the carburetor to atomize gas is different not only in each makers' product but also in the manufacturers' own products and in models of the same car. In one year's production run of the same car you may find several different carbuertor changes.

Faced with a situation like this, it is difficult in a book of this kind to tell you precisely what to do in any specific case. However, all carburetors end up doing the same thing. If you know what they should be doing, you can trace back and find out what is wrong.

Carburetors look bewilderingly complicated. Yet when you tear down your first one in an automobile repair class, you are generally surprised at how basically simple the things really are.

However, tearing down a carburetor piece by piece comes under the heading of advanced tune-ups. With modern detergent gasolines you don't need to "boil out" a carb (that is, tear it down and clean the insides) as often as formerly. Generally you won't need a boil out more than once every 50,000 miles.

To explain the teardown and reassembly of the bewildering number of carb variations would take an entire library. One manufacturer in his technical manual uses space equal to one-third of this book just to explain the differences in carburetors on a single year's models. The Carter Carburetor Company takes a book bigger than this to explain their models, and naturally it doesn't include the Rochester, Stromberg, and Holley, made by other companies.

Although this diversity and variety may complicate disassembly, boil out, and carburetor repair, it doesn't affect tune-up. All the work we need to do for basic tune-up can be done on the *outside* of the carburetor. It would help if you can find the manufacturer's technical service manual in your local library, but it isn't essential.

The Air Cleaner

The first essential of good carburetion is air. Hot rodders call it "breathing" and spend a lot of money assuring that plenty of air gets into their mills. While we discussed only a single fuel circuit in explaining how the carburetor works, actually there are six individual circuits inside the carburetor. Many of them work through small passages and tiny jets, so that dirt and contamination in the gasoline or air can plug up passages very quickly. When it does, any number of things can happen. Your circuits are

- *Idle Speed Circuit.* This feeds gas to the carburetor when your car is idling and for speeds up to about 20 mph.

When gum gets into this circuit you often have stalling when you stop at a light, and poor acceleration when you start off.

- *Part-throttle Power System.* This circuit operates with a rise in vacuum as the car approaches the limit of the idle system. It allows more liquid fuel to flow into the venturi.
- *Power Enrichment System.* When you get up to high speed or working under a stiff load, such as climbing a steep grade, the power enrichment system comes into play. It gives you a richer air/fuel mixture for increased power.
- *Accelerating Pump circuit.* This is in the carburetor to give an extra squirt of fuel at times like the switch over from the low-speed (idle) circuit to the part-throttle power circuit, and when you have to tramp hard on the throttle in an emergency. You might say its job is to lend a helping hand in an emergency when the other circuits can't give you enough gas.
- *Float Circuit.* This circuit has already been explained. It meters the amount of gas that flows into the float bowl, maintaining the proper level. If the level is too high, gas flows out of the bowl onto the engine with danger of fire. If it is too low, then fuel in the line (jet) extending into the venturi will be too low for the vacuum to suck it into the venturi. (To be scientifically correct, a car vacuum does not "suck." It lowers pressure at one point so that normal atmospheric pressure pushes from the other end.)
- *Choke Circuit.* The choke is nothing but a trapdoor in the air horn that cuts off some of the air coming into the carburetor. It enriches the air/fuel mixture when the engine is cold and additional fuel is needed to keep it going.

These circuits and your engine as a whole are protected by an air cleaner that sits on top of the carburetor air horn and strains dirt and debris from the air coming into the carburetor.

Types of Air Cleaners

If you have an older car, say one built before 1956 or thereabouts, you may have an oil bath type of cleaner. In the bottom of the cleaner there is a shallow pool of engine oil that must be kept filled to an indicated level line. Air comes in the bottom of this type of cleaner; blows across the oil, which picks up particles from the air; and then goes upward through a mesh before being sucked into the carburetor horn. Too much oil in this type of cleaner restricts air to the carburetor.

Since 1956 cars went to the corrugated paper air cleaners. This is serviced as a unit. You must take out the paper cartridge

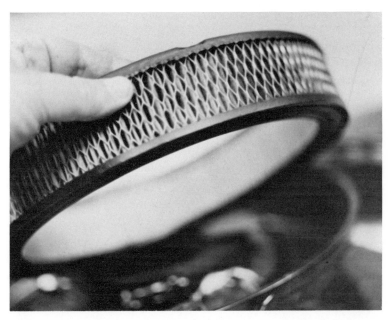

The paper cartridge for an air cleaner is encased in a metal and mesh frame. It can be bumped against the concrete to remove loose dirt and lengthen its use but cannot be satisfactorily cleaned. It must be replaced at tune-up time.

and replace it with a new one. The paper is porous to air and the dirt sticks to the outside. This type of air cleaner is very effective and simple to service.

Servicing the Corrugated Paper Air Cleaner

Maintaining a clean air cleaner is extremely important. As grit and grime pile up on the porous paper, less and less air can get into the carburetor. When this happens you are cutting down on the air in your air/fuel mixture. This makes the engine run richer than it should and this imbalance increases as the air cleaner gets dirtier.

It is no help to adjust the air/fuel ratio for your engine carefully and then upset the whole balance with a dirty air cleaner. The paper cartridge cannot be cleaned. The old oil bath cleaner (and before it the steel wool mesh cleaner) could be washed in kerosene and reoiled for continued use. The paper cartridge cleaner can only be replaced with a new cartridge.

To replace, you have only to remove the top of the air cleaner container on top of the carb. Generally this can be done by loosening a single wing nut and taking off the top plate. Then you pick up the old cartridge, wipe out the inside of the container, and drop the new one in. Replace the top cover and wing nut. That's all. Two minutes' labor. There are exceptions, of course. The large engine for the Ford Pinto requires removing several bolts to get to its air cleaner.

While the cartridge is replaced with each tune-up, in between it is often a good idea to take the cartridge out and bump the flat side of the metal ring that encircles the bottom and top against the garage floor. You can knock out a considerable amount of dirt that way.

Since 1963, when crankcase-ventilating smog-control systems came into use, some cars pick up the emissions from the crankcase and channel them through a hose back to the air cleaner, where they are burned again. You can generally tell if your car is this type because a rubber hose will run from the valve cover on top of the engine to the side of the cleaner container. Although these control systems have a wire mesh filter in the end of the hose when it enters the air cleaner, still considerable varnish and oily substances get through. They shorten the life of your filter. The filter in the control line should be removed when you change the paper filter cartridge. It is replaceable. Wash it in kerosene or solvent and stick it back in the end of the hose.

Cleaning the Carburetor

The air cleaner cleans the air going into the carburetor and a filter and/or sediment bowl cleans the gasoline before it comes into the float bowl. But even so, the car's small passages get gummed up with varnishes and sediments just the same.

The only solution is to clean the carb occasionally. Modern detergent gasolines help keep a carb clean by preventing caking up of gasoline additives in the small circuit passages and circuit jets.

Cleaning a carb ("boiling it out") involves removing it from the car, disassembly, soaking in a powerful cleaner and then washing in solvent to remove the cleaner. Next you blow out the passages with compressed air. It takes from 45 minutes to a couple of hours, depending upon the complications of the carb and the strength of the solvent. Boiling out a carb is not a job for a beginner. Fortunately it is necessary only about every 50,000 miles, so it does not come under normal basic tune-up.

What you can do is use one of the many carburetor-cleaner solutions you'll find on the auto supply store shelves. If your carb isn't in too bad a shape they will work quite well.

Using Carb Cleaner Solvent

There are a number of good brands of carburetor cleaner on the market. Each can has instructions printed on it telling you how to go about using the particular product. They all work about the same, but there may be slight differences and you should follow directions exactly.

In *general* you go about it like this:

1. Remove air cleaner.
2. Start the engine and speed it up to 1,500 rpm. With car specs setting idling speeds from 500 to 800 rpm or more, this means you double the idling speed. If you have a dwell/tach meter, you can easily determine your rpm. You get the faster rpm speed by moving the linkage by hand, speeding up the engine.
3. With the engine turning over at a fast idle, you begin pouring the solvent into the carb's open throat. Pour slowly, keeping your thumb over the hole in the can to adjust the flow.
4. You can expect the engine to slow down and want to stop because the solvent is not a fuel and is not burning and you're upsetting the air/fuel ration by pouring it into the air stream. You keep it running by opening the throttle a little more. If you have to open the throttle more than halfway to keep the car from stalling, then ease up on the amount of solvent you are pouring into the car.
5. Some manufacturers then recommend you dump the final inch or so solvent left in the can into the carb fast enough to stall the engine. The solvent is then left to soak for an hour to loosen carbon in the manifold, around the valves and in the cylinders. Then you start the engine again after the soaking and take it out for a highway run with short burst of wide-open throttle to blast out the carbon.

Carbs are easy to remove. Disconnect all springs and throttle and choke connections to the engine. Then you have only to loosen four bolts to lift it off. This shows a typical V-8 engine set for a carburetor. The four studs in each corner A hold the carb in place. B is the linkage to the throttle which connects with the foot feed in the driver's compartment. The two holes, C, each connecting with one barrel of the two-barrel carb, lead to the intake manifolds of the V-8 engine. If you remove a carb like this, always cover the holes to insure that no debris falls inside that can be sucked into the cylinders. On the V-8 engine the carb sits between the two banks of cylinders.

After a carburetor has been soaked the prescribed time in cleaner, it is washed off in solvent before reassembly. A "boil-out" like this should not be necessary more than once in 50,000 miles.

Now this does work, but we are hesitant to recommend the highway blasts to a beginner. For one thing, if the car is badly carboned up, you can very quickly get "splash fouling" of your plugs. This is when the loosened varnishes and carbon hit your sparkplug electrodes and stick. This can ruin your plugs. If they were going to be replaced, as they should be at tune-up time, this is no great loss. But if the fouling stalls your engine on the middle of a freeway or turnpike, you are indeed in a poor place to undertake a cleaning job.

We'd say you are better off just to goose the throttle a few times in your garage (plenty of ventilation, please).

Also, these bursts of wide-open throttle have been known to blow holes in the old muffler when the engine backfires. It could happen to you. But then you probably needed a new one anyway!

Cleaner used in this manner cleans the throat of the carburetor and helps get rid of carbon in the intake manifold, around the valves, and in the cylinders. However, it does not penetrate into the inner passages of the carb itself. Modern detergent gasolines, as we mentioned earlier, do a very good job of keeping carburetor passages clean. There was a time when we had to clean a carburetor every six months. However, some gum still forms more or less frequently.

Where does this gum and varnish come from, and why don't the gas filters keep it out? It comes from evaporation of gas in the carburetor, which leaves behind substances that don't evaporate.

Cleaner in the Gas Tank

If your carburetor does get gummed up despite the cleaner in your gasoline, you can try adding carburetor cleaner to the gas in your tank. Directions on the can tell you how to go about it. Generally you add a can to a tank of gasoline. You must add the cleaner to the gas. Don't put the cleaner in an empty tank and fill up with gas. Be sure you have at least 10 gallons in the tank. It cleans while you drive, but you'll probably have some rough idling while the cleaner is in the tank.

One company makes a kit so you can tap your gas line and feed the cleaner directly into the carb. Some service stations can do this for you, if you lack the experience. It's relatively inexpensive and might save you the price of an expensive "boil out."

Adjusting Your Carburetor

There are two adjustments to make on a simple tune-up. These are setting the *idle speed* and the *idle-speed fuel mixture*. We mentioned before that a carburetor has six circuits, each of which handle the amount of fuel going through the carb at different speeds and conditions. We mentioned that the rush of air through the carb throat pulls gas by vacuum out of the jet running to the float bowl.

This is true for normal-speed operations, but not true at idle and speeds below 20 miles per hour. You see, when you step on the foot throttle in the driver's compartment you are not opening up the fuel line to give more gas, but instead are turning the air valve in the carburetor throat. If you let in more air it naturally sucks more gas out of the float bowl, so for practical purposes you are stepping on the gas when you push down on the floor throttle.

But at idle speed the throttle valve in the carb is *closed*. Therefore there is no rush of air to pull gas into the air stream. So we have an entirely different circuit that bypasses the one we use to scoot along the highway. This *idle* or *low-speed circuit* furnishes gas through a different idle jet to keep the car running when there is not sufficient air coming in to operate the high-speed circuit.

The jets for the high-speed system are fixed and cannot be adjusted, unless for hop-up reasons, in which case you change the jets entirely. Hop-up may be illegal if it increases smog emissions.

The air/fuel ratio in the idle circuit is controlled by the idle-mixture screw. This is a needle valve that adjusts the flow in the circuit. Screwing the idle-mixture screw thins out or *leans* the air/fuel ratio, providing less gas. Screwing it out makes the mixture *richer,* providing more gas for the amount of air.

Again, smog control has complicated carburetor adjustments. Once this mixture was adjusted for the smoothest idle. Now it is adjusted for the leanest possible idle—in other words, as lean as you can get it and still get the engine to idle without stalling.

This is the procedure for adjusting the idle mixture when you don't have a vacuum gauge.

1. After setting dwell and timing, with engine at normal operating temperature, disconnect vacuum advance hose at *distributor* and plug the hose. Also remove vacuum hose at air cleaner if the car is so equipped, and plug opening. If the car has a vacuum-release parking brake, follow manufacturer's recommendations.

2. Be sure hand brake is applied firmly.

3. Final idle settings should always be made with the air cleaner in place, for this will take into account any restrictions on air flow caused by the cleaner. Otherwise, you might find the mixture richer if you adjust with the cleaner off and then put it on again. If you are not completely familiar with your carburetor, it might be well to remove the air cleaner and get acquainted with the positions of the idle adjustments before starting. Sometimes with big air cleaners and jammed-in smog accessories, you can't always see the adjusting screws and must proceed by feel. So it pays to know where they are.

4. Often the curb-idle adjustment (for speed) and the idle

mixture adjustment (for air/fuel ratio) look alike. Generally, if you don't have the manufacturer's manual for your car, you can tell by its position. The mixture screw leads into the body of the carb, while the idle-speed adjusting screw is generally on the throttle linkage. The idea of the mixture screw is to enlarge or reduce the passage inside the carburetor. The purpose of the idle-speed screw is to keep the throttle cracked open so that screwing it in just keeps the throttle from closing. With these purposes in mind, you should be able to determine which is which by inspecting your carb. If not, all you can do is refer to the manual for your car.

Setting the Idle Mixture

5. On older cars use a tachometer to set the idle speed to specifications. (See below for instruction on how to set idle speed.) Then with the engine at specified idle, screw in the idle-mixture screw until you start losing rpm because the engine is starving for gas. Next, back off from this too lean position until you start losing rpm and get rough idling from too rich a mixture. Then back off from this to the best performance between the two.

6. On smog-controlled and later cars you'll have to make the setting according to specs. From 1970 on, these should *be on a decal under the hood of your car.* For previous years you go to the specification sheets. If the mixture-adjusting screw has a limiter cap, then you must confine your adjustments within this range.

7. Don't forget to reconnect any vacuum lines you disconnected and plugged after you get through adjusting the idle mixture and the curb-idle speed.
   On some new carburetors the fuel mixture is preset and cannot be changed.

Setting the Idle Speed

The curb-idle speed-adjusting screw is on the throttle assembly by the side of the carburetor. Screwing it down merely keeps the throttle from closing all the way. To adjust the curb idle, hook up the tachometer or tach/dwell meter the same way you did to check dwell, but push the switch on the tach/-dwell meter to the tach setting. That is, connect the red lead to the distributor side of the coil and the other lead to ground. Look up the specs to see what the idle speed should be. This will vary according to whether you have a standard shift or an automatic shift, and according to the natural dirtiness of the engine. Dirty engines sometimes have to idle faster than more clean-burning engines in order to reduce pollutants. Specs on all new engines are set higher than older engines.

Checking Out the Choke

If you look through the throat of a carburetor, you will see two flat metal discs hinged on a rod. One disc is above the venturi (narrow throat of the carburetor) and the other is below it. The lower disc is the throttle valve which turns to cut off the flow of air through the air horn to regulate the amount of fuel that gets to the cylinders.

The top disc or valve is the choke. The choke plate can also be turned like the throttle plate to cut off air coming into the carburetor. Both valves do the same thing—they restrict air— but since they are in different locations the result of their air restriction is different. The throttle valve is below the venturi, and gasoline, for normal-speed operations, has already been mixed with the air before it reaches the throttle valve. (This does not apply to the idle circuit, which is below the throttle valve since it must supply fuel when the engine speed has been cut by the throttle closing.)

The choke valve is above the venturi. It shuts off air before

On this particular model the idle air/fuel mixture is adjusted with this spring-loaded screw. Later models will have a limiter cap so that you cannot adjust beyond certain limits. Other points of interest are A, air/fuel idle mixture set screw; B, fuel inlet; C, float bowl; D, automatic choke housing; E, idle-speed set screw; F, air horn. This is a Carter one-barrel carburetor.

it reaches the venturi where vacuum mixes the air with gasoline. It never, of course, completely shuts off the air, or the engine would not run. When a carb is torn down for repair, we use a gauge to adjust the choke valve so it never closes beyond this point.

This cutting down on the air upsets the normal air/fuel ratio, resulting in less air and more gas. The mixture is then "richer." We need this richer mixture to start a cold engine. So the engine is "choked," which means that we close the choker valve to reduce the air intake and thus enrich the fuel mixture. This is because the elements that make up gasoline have different boiling points. Some of them are below the temperature of a cold engine, and much more gasoline is needed to start the cold engine than will be necessary when the engine warms up to operating temperature.

At one time the choke was manually operated from the

dashboard by pulling up on a cable that closed the choke valve on the carb. The driver had to know his car to operate it successfully so he could partially open and then completely open the choke at the right time. Now we have automatic chokes to do the work for us. Sometimes they get clogged up, so checking out the automatic choke is very much a part of a good tune-up job.

In automatic chokes, a lever that operates the opening and closing of the choke plate is connected to a bimetallic spring. This coil spring, made of two different types of metals, tightens up when it is cold. This tightening pulls the lever and closes the choke valve in the carburetor air horn. There is a pipe running from the choke-spring housing to the manifold that directs hot air from a "heat stove" up into the choke-spring housing. As the spring warms up, it gradually opens up and pushes the choke valve open, permitting a normal flow of air through the carburetor.

Types of Automatic Chokes

All types of automatic chokes work on the principle of the bimetallic spring, but they differ in where this spring is located. On older types of cars the spring is located in a bakelite housing on the side of the carburetor. Adjusting notches are pro-

On this Carter carb the automatic choke cover is removed by loosening four screws and lifting the cover straight off. The air cleaner fits around the ledge A. B is the fuel inlet, C the idle-speed adjusting screw, D the idle-speed fuel-mixture screw.

On this two-barrel carb there are two fuel mixture screws to adjust. This view is from the bottom of the carburetor after it has been removed from the car. This is a Carter ball-and-ball type.

vided so that the leanness or richness of the choke can be changed by rotating the Bakelite cap one or two notches. Loosening the four retaining screws permits the cap to be removed for cleaning. The accompanying photograph shows the cover removed on a Carter carb. The bimetallic spring is inside the cap and is not removed. All you need to do is insure that all moving parts are not binding. If they don't move freely, then squirt some spray-type carburetor or automatic choke cleaner inside, work them loose, and wipe the inside clean. Also check the outside linkage for binding in the same way. When you put the cover back on, be sure that the hook of the spring wraps around the operating lever so that it will work the choke plate.

The only other thing to check is whether carbon or varnish gum has obstructed the hot-air pipe. There may be a screen inside the pipe to keep debris from getting into the choke housing. If so, see that it is clean. Wash it out with solvent or kerosene.

In the second type of automatic choke, which is becoming more common, the bimetallic spring is in a heat well in the manifold directly below the carburetor. A heavy wire link connects the spring with the choke-operating lever on the carb. You can find the well by tracing along the extended linkage running down from the choke.

In this kind of setup you adjust the richness or leanness of the choke by bending the linkage slightly to lengthen or shorten it. However, it is very seldom that you will need to do this. Maintenance at tune-up time includes checking the parts for binding and cleaning the screen in the hot-air passage. If the choke plate does not open fully for a warm engine and close to the specified gap on a cold one, you adjust the linkage as mentioned above.

The Heat Riser

Trouble with the heat riser is one of the most common sources of poor car performance, yet this component is the most easily overlooked. The heat riser is a valve located at the bottom of the exhaust manifold where the exhaust pipe joins the manifold. It looks like a choke valve and is operated by a bimetallic temperature-sensitive spring just as the choke is.

When the engine is cold, the spring closes the valve and hot air is forced up through two holes to the carburetor to help it warm up fast. As the engine heats up and the extra heat is no longer needed, the bimetallic spring loosens and a weight on the heat riser opens the valve.

This valve carbons up very easily, generally sticking in the open position so that no heat rises to the carburetor. In this case you will generally have stalling of the car until the engine heats up.

You also get stalling in a similar manner when you stop at lights when the low-speed jets are stopped up in the carburetor. The way you tell the difference is that if the fuel jets are the trouble the stalling will continue to occur when the engine gets hot. The heat riser affects the cold engine only.

One type of automatic choke housed in a Bakelite covered compartment on the carb. It can be adjusted by loosening the cover and turning it a notch or two according to the scale A. B the choke plate inside the air horn of the carburetor, C the idle adjustment and D the idle-mixture screw. This is a Carter one-barrel carb.

How to Open a Stuck Heat Riser

You check the heat riser by putting your hand under the exhaust manifold. (Be sure that the engine is cold—No point in frying your hand on the hot manifold.) Find the weighted lever that operates the heat riser. You probably can't see it and must operate by feel. You should be able to work the weighted lever back and forth easily. If not, then spray around it with carburetor cleaner and work the lever back and forth until it moves freely. If it's stuck so badly you can't move it by hand, tap it with a hammer back and forth until the solvent works its way into the valve and loosens it up for you.

On much older cars you may find that loosening a stuck heat riser doesn't cure the cold-engine stalling, yet checking out other possibilities is also ineffective. Generally the trouble is that the holes running from the heat riser up to the carburetor seat have become completely jammed with carbon. The only solution is to remove the carburetor and punch out the holes.

Incidentally, it is O.K. to "punch out" these holes, but never

In this type of automatic choke the clip on the end of the bimetallic spring A fits over the upraised lever B to operate the choker plate inside the carburetor throat. C is the hot-air inlet.

poke anything into the passages of a carburetor. Always soak out carb circuits with solvent and then blow them out with compressed air. Carb jets are carefully measured to give the correct fuel/air ratio, and poking them with wires and/or needles to get out obstructions may enlarge the jets and upset the ratio. Then you'll wonder why you can't tune the thing no matter what you do.

Chapter 12

SMOG DEVICES

Automobile smog was once just a Southern California problem. It has now become a national problem. New York now has a mandatory smog inspection program for vehicles for hire. Chicago has a smog test program. So does the state of New Jersey. Even a clear-air state like Colorado has programs under test to insure that automobile smog will not become a problem in the future. Currently the Environmental Protection Agency has ordered that all 1975 and later cars sold in California be equipped with catalytic converter mufflers as a *national test*. If it proves successful in eliminating oxides of nitrogen, it will later be required on all cars everywhere.

The trouble has been that smog devices have definitely reduced car performance, but they are something that has to be lived with.

PCV System

The first system adopted to control automobile emissions was the Positive Crankcase Ventilation System, or PCV. When a car operates, small amounts of combustion gases "blow by" the rings into the crankcase. When a car is choked during cold starts, some of the gas may not vaporize, or may condense out of the vapor and drip past the rings. Also, water forms in the cylinders as a by-product of combustion. All of these drop down into the crankcase, and they have to be removed to keep them from clogging up the oil, which would cause damage to the bearings.

This unwanted hydrocarbon material was once vented into the air to get it out of the crankcase. The drive on smog control stopped this, and a Positive Crankcase Ventilation System was added by law to our engines. All it does is pipe the vapors from the crankcase to the intake manifold, where they are sucked back into the engine and the unburned portions reburned.

The only regular maintenance needed on the PCV system at tune-up time is checking the hose that runs from the rocker arm cover either to the intake manifold just below the carburetor or, in certain cars, to the air cleaner. Check the hose for breaks or for poor connections at the end. You'll also have to check and possibly replace the PCV valve. It is located at the grommet end of the hose going into the rubber grommet on the rocker arm cover. Pull the hose out of the grommet and detach the valve from the end of the hose. The valve is now

An increasingly common sight on the California street is this State Highway Patrol vehicle emissions test. Here a patrolman inserts a probe in the car's exhaust and the emissions are read by another patrolman from the dials of an exhaust analyzer.

The PCV valve fits into the end of the hose held by the mechanic's hand. It is inserted in the rubber grommet indicated by the arrow. This is a V-8 Chevrolet.

of one-piece construction and cannot be opened for cleaning. Inside there is a spring-loaded plunger against which suction or vacuum in the line works. At idle speed, when vacuum is greatest and crank case blowby is least, the valve regulates the vacuum.

Cleaning the PCV Valve

When PCV systems were first introduced about 1963 we were told to clean them periodically. Now we are instructed that we should not clean them at all, but instead replace them at tune-up intervals. It is difficult to understand why we can't spray the inside with carburetor cleaner, soak for a while, and then blow out the valve with compressed air from a tire pump. But the people who make them say you shouldn't. So regardless of the logic we recommend that you do as the manufacturers say, because they surely know best.

You can buy a tester that fits over your oil filler hole that can tell you if your PCV valve is clogged. Generally a clogged valve will cause rough idling. However, a lot of things can cause an engine to idle rough. If you don't have a tester, try removing the oil filler cap. Hold your hand over it and see if you feel a slight suction. If so, you're O.K. If not, check for kinks in the hose before you rush out to buy a new valve. The cheapest tester you can buy is about $4, and you can get replacement valves for about a dollar if you go to a supply house instead of the parts department of a car dealer, who may charge about 50 percent more. Unless you are doing a lot of work for the neighbors, it is hardly worth the money to get a tester. You'll be better off to just buy a new valve.

Air Injection

One of the reasons for smog-producing exhaust emissions is that all the hydrocarbons (gasoline) are not burned in the cylinders. These hydrocarbons pass out the exhaust into the air, where the action of sunlight upon the particles in the air produces the eye-irritating smog. One system to handle this is "air injection"—or Thermacter, as Ford calls their version. In this system there is an air pump that runs off the fan belt. This pump forces fresh air through a bypass valve to an air manifold assembly mounted on the exhaust manifold. This fresh air hits the exhausting gases from the cylinder to help complete full combustion or burning of the unburned gas in the exhaust.

All you can do on these systems is check and clean the filter, make sure the air pump is working, check the tension on the belt that drives the pump, and see that the check valve is operative. The check valve prevents exhaust from driving the fresh air back into the pump under certain conditions.

Evaporation Control Systems

A car doesn't have to run to pollute the air. Even when the motor is dead there is evaporation of gasoline both in the gas tank and in the float bowl of the carb. This sends hydrocarbons into the air, where the sun turns them into smog.

To stop this, car makers have come up with evaporative control systems. One such system uses activated charcoal canisters. The canister is a small tank filled with charcoal particles. The evaporative fumes from the tank and carburetor float bowl are carried to the intake manifold to be burned when the car is running; but when it is stopped, the fumes go to the canister, where the activated charcoal filters out the hydrocarbons and lets the purified air out through a filter at the bottom.

In this type of system, all you can do at tune-up time is replace the filter in the bottom of the canister at 12,000-mile intervals.

Chrysler has a system that stores the fumes in the crankcase until the engine is started, whereupon the fumes are shunted to the intake manifold to be burned.

Heated Air System

Federal clean-air requirements have forced new cars to operate on leaner fuel mixtures, which in turn has caused a decrease in performance at low temperatures. This has led some car makers to go to a heated air system in the air cleaner to improve performance during warm-up. You might call it a sort of elaborate heat riser. There is a snorkel tube on the air cleaner and a trapdoor inside that is controlled by a temperature sensor in the air cleaner. If your car's temperature is below 85° F when you start it, the sensor will cause a door to close in the snorkel, which lets air for the carburetor come up through a hot-air pipe from the "heat stove" on the exhaust manifold. The exhaust manifold, catching the hot gases from cylinder combustion, heats up as soon as the engine starts. The resulting hot-air flow to the carburetor helps the cold engine run better on the lean carburetor mixtures during the warm-up phase. (Sometimes in cold weather the gas in the fuel vapor has a tendency to condense back out of the vapor.) As soon as the engine reaches operating temperature, the door in the snorkel cuts off the flow of hot air and the carburetor receives normal ambient air.

Tune-up for these thermostatically controlled air cleaners consists of checking the door in the snorkel. It should be open, if the temperature is below 85 degrees, but should close when the car starts. When the engine warms, it should open again. All you can check for is binding of any working parts. Otherwise, it is a service-station job, since replacing the vacuum motor that operates the door requires drilling out spot welds.

Catalyst Mufflers

Catalyst mufflers are going to be standard equipment on most cars in the immediate future. A catalyst is a substance that causes or speeds up a chemical change without undergoing a permanent change itself. In catalyst mufflers platinum or palladium acts as the catalyst to change exhaust hydrocarbons into carbon dioxide and water. They are very expensive and can be ruined by leaded gasoline.

A recent press release from General Motors said: "GM is considering using the [catalyst] converters on all its 1975 cars. . . . The system includes an electronic ignition and a new type carburetor."

The electronic distributors will be somewhat like the ones discussed earlier, except they will have the centrifugal advance above the reluctor like the current contact points on GM distributors. GM said their system would carry about 20,000 *more* volts across the plugs than the regular ignition system. It will also have a wider sparkplug gap. "This," says GM, "will give us spark energy three times as long as we get in a conventional system," meaning that you'll hold the "match" to fuel longer, starting a fire quicker in the cylinder.

Not much was said about the new carburetor, except that

"it has a lot of the characteristics of air metering that you have with fuel injection but it's more accurate. It will be a one-barrel affair."

All this will make tune-ups easier.

Chapter 13

A CHECK LIST FOR TUNING A CAR

An automobile engine is not really complicated once you understand how it works. But when you are just starting and someone keeps throwing a mass of new terms at you, you can be excused for getting bewildered.

In order to avoid adding more confusion, we have started with the battery and followed straight through the ignition system to the sparkplugs and then to the carburetor. In actually tuning your car you might not follow this exact sequence. You need to set certain things before others. We followed the straight sequence in our discussion in order to avoid adding confusion by jumping from ignition to carburetor and back again several times. Therefore, we are including here a standard tune-up sequence. This is a check list only. For specific details, check the index and refer back to our basic discussion.

Where to Begin?

Most tune-up check sheets start with the battery. This is logical, since the battery is where the ignition begins. However, I prefer to start with tune-up solvent in the carburetor—

152

if I'm going to use it. I like to use it first before I set timing, clean plugs and the rest, so that if I get splash fouling on the plugs I don't have to go back and clean them.

When we speak of using carburetor cleaner here, we are talking about pouring it in the carb throat. You should not use carburetor cleaner in your gas tank during a tune-up. The solvent causes rough idling when used in the gas and this can upset your adjustments during tune-up. If you need this kind of cleaner, pour it in the tank, use up the entire tank and refill with fresh gas when you start your normal tune-up.

You can pour tune-up solvent through the carburetor or use the method that puts the solvent directly into the carburetor fuel inlet just before a tune-up, for then the solvent goes right through the engine. It is not mixed with an entire tank of gas.

With this out of the way, let's begin the sequence:

Check the Battery

Use a hydrometer if you can't afford more expensive battery test equipment. Remember the hydrometer is affected by temperature. If you don't have an hydrometer, you can tell whether your battery is O.K. if it turns the starter easily, and if your lights are bright and do not dim too much when you hit the starter. If the starter is sluggish and the lights get dim, a hydrometer test will show if the battery is discharged. If battery specific gravity is good, check for poor connections or broken cables and wires.

Check Battery Connections

Check cables to ground and to the starter. Clean off battery acid with a solution of baking soda and water. Acid will foam and then can be washed off. Dry top of battery. Use puller to take off cables. Clean posts and inside of terminal connectors with wire brushes. Replace and tighten connections.

Check Wiring

Begin with the battery cables, following wiring through to starter, coil, distributor, and sparkplugs. Look for loose connections, broken wires, cracked insulation, cracked boots, and oil-soaked wires. Replace wires if necessary. Broken wires can be detected by using a test lamp. Clamp the leads to each end of the wire under test. If electricity is flowing through, the lamp will light.

Replace Sparkplugs

If you don't know how to rewire your plugs according to the firing order, then mark each sparkplug wire with a piece of tape and a number when you remove it, so you can get it back right. Use care in removing the wire to avoid breaking the conductor inside. Use a deep socket to remove the plugs. If rear plugs or those hidden under air conditioners and smog devices are hard to get to, use extensions or universal joints on your sparkplug wrench. Plugs to be replaced or cleaned can be removed one at a time and replaced immediately to avoid any mix-up in getting the wires back in place. In replacing plugs, use only the numbered plug your specs call for. However, if the plug you remove is a different spec, *and your car has been performing satisfactorily,* a previous mechanic may have made the change because his tests showed that you needed a different heat range of plug.

Check Compression

While the plugs are out, check compression with a compression gauge. Follow manufacturer's recommendations on its use, referring to your specs for the correct psi (pounds per square inch) pressure for your car. Poor compression indicates internal engine trouble. An engine with poor compression cannot be satisfactorily tuned. You have bad rings, scored cylinder walls, poor seating valves or burned valves.

Gapping Plugs

After making the compression check, regap your sparkplugs. Even though a plug is new and of the correct size and heat range for your car, it does not follow that the gap is necessarily right. Check and reset. If possible, use a torque wrench to tighten the plugs correctly. Overtightening can strip threads or stretch metal so that your gap is incorrect. Take care that distributor wires are put on the right plugs according to the engine's firing order.

Check Distributor Cap

Remove cap from distributor, check for cracks, corrosion, pitted or burned connections and "carbon tracks." Carbon tracks are black streaks running between terminal connections, indicating a short circuit. If inserts and contacts are in bad shape, replace the cap. If the old cap is to be reused, clean insert connections inside the wire towers on top. Use a small round wire brush. Clean terminals inside cap as well. Clean all grease and dirt from top and inside of cap. When you remove wires from the towers, be sure to mark wire and tower so that you can get them back right.

Check Ignition Rotor

If the contacts (in center for current from coil and tip where the rotor connects with the inserts to send the juice to the plugs) are not burned and pitted, rotor can be used again. However, standard tune-up kits come with contact points set, condenser and new rotor. Get the right kit for your car.

Replace Points and Condenser

In removing the old contact points and condenser, pay close attention to the way the primary circuit wire and the condenser wire are connected together, so that you can get them back right. Remove points and condenser and replace with new set from tune-up kit.

(Instructors do not agree on whether a beginner should remove the distributor from the car to work on it. Some think a beginner has enough to worry about without adding the complications of possibly getting the distributor back in wrong. It is much easier to work on if removed from the car, and if your distributor is in an awkward position where you can't get to it, you may be forced to remove it from the car. If you must remove it, see Appendix A for instructions on how to get it back in right.)

Adjust Distributor Points

This may be done by adjusting the gap with a feeler gauge to proper specs, or—and this is best—by using a dwell meter. After the dwell has been set, replace distributor cap and check wires for proper seating in the cap and for correct position according to firing order of the car.

Change Air Cleaner Cartridge

Before going to the carburetor, change the air cleaner cartridge if of the paper type, or clean and replace oil bath if of the older type. It is important that the air cleaner be changed before adjusting the carburetor, since a dirty cleaner will restrict air flow into the engine.

Set Initial Timing

Use a timing light, connecting it according to the light manufacturer's instructions. Set the timing with the vacuum advance hose disconnected and plugged. Timing must be set at a specified rpm, so you need to set idle speed on the carburetor by using the tach section of the tach/dwell meter. Timing is adjusted by loosening the hold-down bolt on the distributor and rotating the distributor to bring the timing marks into alignment.

Check Centrifugal and Vacuum Advance

The initial timing is set at a specified idle speed. As the engine speed increases, the ignition has to fire earlier to compensate for the faster-moving crankshaft. You can check the amount of this advance by putting the disconnected vacuum advance hose back on the distributor. Then with the timing light focused on the timing marks, increase the speed of the engine and observe the movement of the timing mark. The timing advance you observe will be the combined advance of the centrifugal advance and the vacuum advance. To find out how much each is advancing the timing, again disconnect the vacuum advance hose and plug it. The amount of advance you then observe under the timing light will be caused by the mechanical centrifugal advance. Subtract the number of degrees of centrifugal advance from the total advance you observed with both operating and you get the amount of vacuum advance. Compare these figures with specifications for your engine. Some of the spec sheets you buy in parts stores do not give the advance specs. If you can't obtain a shop manual on your car from the library, then write the Customer Relations Department of the car manufacturer and ask for them. If the advance curves are not to spec, then it probably means that dirt, rust, or grease is causing the weights to stick. Part of your tests should be to insure that the weight moves freely when you replace points. If the trouble is not caused by binding, then the trouble is probably in the weight springs. They may be too weak. Remember—*and this is extremely important*—that initial timing sets the pace for all the rest. If your initial (idle speed) timing is off, then everything else along the advance curve will be wrong also. You must get your original initial timing within specs.

Check Carburetor

Check the linkage for binding or too loose throttle; check the automatic choke for free operation; check the heat riser for sticking. Look for leaks and make sure the carburetor hold down bolts are tight. Remove for "boil out" if necessary.

Adjust Carburetor

Adjust the idle mixture and reset the idle speed. In some cars there is an extra idle-speed adjustment, called the fast-idle adjustment, in addition to the regular curb-idle adjustment. In other cars the two are combined. The curb idle gives you your regular idle speed, but when the car is cold you may need additional, faster idle speed to keep the car from stalling. When you set the automatic choke by pressing down on the accelerator before you start, this also pushes on a cam that presses against the fast-idle adjusting screw to open the throttle wider. As the choke opens, this cam moves slowly, closing the extra idle-speed action. In some cars there is only one adjusting screw. The action of the cam provides the higher-speed change for cold starts. In any case, if you are adjusting the fast idle, it must be done with the adjusting screw on the high point of the fast-idle cam.

Final Checks

Before completing the tune-up, check and tighten the fan belt, radiator hoses, and smog hoses and devices.

Chapter 14

WHAT'S NEXT?

This book is an introduction to automobile tune-ups, aimed at the beginner. Its purpose is to ease him over the more confusing parts of automobile electricity and carburetion. As a result a lot has *not* been said. Once the beginner has mastered the basic principles of engine tune-up, he should keep studying advanced engine tuneup.

Here we have dealt primarily with an engine in good condition and have told how to make necessary adjustments to keep it in tune. Little was said about how to repair things that are wrong. This was done for two reasons. (1) Tune-up is not automobile repair, and if you take a car in for tune-up only the mechanic will follow a set schedule of adjustments. He will not repair various troubles unless you pay extra and make a separate work request. (2) Our purpose was to provide a foundation for basic tune-up. We could not go into the hundred-and-one repair methods without ending up with an encyclopedia. Also, any turn-offs onto repair would only make the job of learning basic tune-ups still more confusing.

If you learn basic tune-ups, you have the foundation upon which to build your knowledge of both advanced tune-up and automobile repair as a whole. We must all crawl before we can walk, and toddle before we can run.

Too many budding mechanics don't know this, which is the reason why there are so many poor professional mechanics today. They learned *part* of their job and not all of it. They are not well grounded in the total picture. Too often they are doing things without knowing why. This is very true of backyard mechanics. They learn one thing but often do not understand all the other factors that go to make that thing work. I know of one such mechanic who has been changing his points for years but never knew how they really worked. He argued that the current to fire the plugs went through the points. Actually, it is the primary current, which controls the formation of the electromagnetic field in the coil, that goes through the points. The current to fire the plugs is induced in the secondary circuit by the breaking of the primary current by the points.

So why does he need to know this when he can change his points satisfactorily, gap them correctly, and get the car moving again because someone once showed him how? Because knowing *how* permits you to do only the job you know how to do. If something goes wrong outside your limited knowledge, you can't figure out *how* without knowing *why*.

Here we have concentrated on the *why* along with a limited amount of *how*. Your job now is to learn more *how*. Without getting into actual complicated automobile repair, there are many things you can do to extend your tune-up practice. Among them are the following.

- Check and simple repair of fuel pumps.
- Check and repair of your starter and alternator systems.
- Use of the vacuum gauge in analyzing an engine. Vacuum gauges are simple to use and can tell you a lot about the operation of an engine.
- Use of the electronic scope for engine analysis. Such scopes aren't cheap, but some are within the average budget.
- Carburetor teardown, cleaning, and use of repair kits.

Every year, of course, brings changes in automobile models. Some are small, some (like the trend toward electronic ignition) are major changes. However, if you understand tune-up principles, you will not have any trouble understanding these new developments.

The Wankel Rotary Engine

One of the most interesting new developments in automotives is the Wankel rotary engine now used in the Mazda automobile. There are hints that some major U.S. manufacturers may be heading toward use of the rotary engine themselves. Also, there are indications that the two-cycle engine used on lawn mowers, motorcycles, and the like may be on their way out, to be replaced by the more efficient Wankel-type rotary engine.

The Wankel replaces the conventional cylinders and pistons with a triangular rotor that revolves in a combustion chamber shaped like a big figure eight. In getting rid of the pistons, the Wankel also eliminated valves, valve rods, valve lifters, the camshaft to operate the valve rods, and the crankshaft. The only moving parts associated inside the engine are the rotors (there are two of these), a balance weight, a flywheel, and a shaft to turn the rotors.

Elimination of so many moving parts removes a very great deal of maintenance trouble.

The rotors are triangular in shape with a depression in each of the three flat surfaces. This depression serves as the piston. There is a seal in each of the three corners of the rotor that locks in the fuel. Fuel is fed into the depression as the engine turns and is compressed by the rotor in turning. Then, as the fuel-filled depression passes the sparkplugs, they fire.

The original Mazda rotary engine had one distributor and one sparkplug for each of the rotors. As a means of smog control (the original Mazda was a very "dirty" engine), the

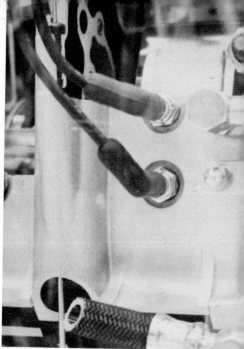

The Mazda engine employs two distributors. There are only three towers on each distributor. One is the high-tension connector to the coil and the other two feed the double "leading" and "trailing" plugs.

The Mazda engine has two sparkplugs for each rotor. The top plug is the "trailing" plug and the bottom one is the "leading" plug. They must be timed separately. Plugs must be a type made for the Mazda so they will penetrate the correct depth into the engine and have the correct heat range.

current production models use two distributors, one for each rotor. And each rotor has two plugs that fire not quite simultaneously for each charge of gas.

Tuning the Mazda

When the Mazda was first introduced to the American market, tune-up specialists were apprehensive. They wondered what extra work they would have to do, and how much schooling they might have to take to learn about this strange new kind of automobile engine.

The answer is that if you understand how and why to tune a standard automobile engine, you can tune a Wankel. You do pretty much the same thing for the same reasons, but in a slightly different way.

You replace and gap your points in the distributor just as you do on the conventional engine. You can use a dwell meter that senses spark impulses on the rotary engine just as on the others. Dwell angle for current Mazda engines is from 55 to 61 degrees.

You inspect your distributor cap for cracks, carbon tracks, and burned connections just as usual. The timing is slightly different owing to the double distributor system. However, timing is adjusted by loosening the distributor hold-down bolt and revolving the distributor just as you do on a Chevvy or Ford.

The Mazda Distributors

The RX-2 is the model that first included the twin distributor system. One distributor is for the plugs on the *leading side.* The second distributor is for the plugs on the *trailing side.* The leading side is the first plug uncovered as the rotor turns. The trailing plug is the second in line. The purpose of the two plugs is to insure that all the fuel is ignited. The reason for the initial reputation of the Mazda as a "dirty" engine was that the single plug could not burn all the fuel at certain speeds, and quite a bit of unburned hydrocarbons went out the exhaust. The firing of the second plug gives a second ignition to burn remaining hydrocarbons. The bottom plug, as viewed from the side of the engine, is the leading plug. The top plug is the trailing plug.

Timing marks for the R-100 and the RX-2 series Mazda rotary engines are notches cut in the V-belt pulley for the fan belt. There is an indicator pin on the engine to align them with. This takes the place of the familiar scales on standard engines. The notches are colored. The yellow notch is the timing mark for the leading plug and the trailing notch is painted orange.

In timing the rotary engine you use the standard timing light. If it is a powered light, connect to the battery (or A-C current if it is an A-C light) in the same manner as with the piston engine, but you connect the lead you formerly used on the

The heart of the Wankel rotary engine is the rotor, a triangular-shaped block with a depression in each of its three sides. This depression is the rotary engine's "piston."

distributor side of the coil for piston engines to the *Number 1 leading plug* of the rotary engine. This is the bottom plug on the side toward the front of the engine.

Timing is set at 700 rpm (900 for the RX-3). The leading plugs are set for 0 degrees before TDC and the trailing plugs are set for 5 degrees *after* TDC. You make only one timing adjustment for the two leading plugs and one for the trailing plugs, since they work from the same distributor. Setting the timing on one sets the timing on the other.

Setting the Mazda Idle Speed

The Mazda carburetor has two throats, and each feeds one of the two rotors in the engine. The idle-speed adjust screw is between the two, and a single adjustment regulates the idle speed to both rotors. Connect a tachometer to the number one leading plug and adjust the idle to 700 rpm for the RX-2 and

900 the RX-3. This adjustment is made before the ignition is timed, but the idle should be rechecked after timing.

The Mazda with the Wankel rotary engine was first introduced into the United States in California but is now being sold in the rest of the nation. The latest information from Mazda is that by 1975 they expect to have 655 dealers in the United States selling 300,000 cars a year. They sold 20,000 here in 1971, 57,850 in 1972, and expect a sale of 120,000 in 1973. In mid 1973 there were 327 dealers nationwide in 36 states.

With the expected increase in sales you will be seeing many more of these revolutionary engines on the road. If you understand the "how" and "why" of basic engine tune-up, you will have no trouble adjusting to the rotary engine when it comes your way. With all the major automobile manufacturers (except Ford) taking an interest in the Wankel, it may come your way sooner than you think.

GLOSSARY

Accelerator   Throttle control.

Air cleaner   Filter for air entering carburetor.

Alternator   An alternating-current generator used to power automobile accessories and to recharge batteries.

Amperes (amperage)   One ampere is the amount or quantity of electricity flowing in a circuit having a one-ohm resistance and a pressure of one volt.

Arcing   The burning caused by electrical current trying to jump a gap.

Automatic choke   A device that automatically adjusts the amount of air flowing into a carburetor. It is operated by a bimetallic spring that contracts with cold and expands with heat.

Ballast resistor   Resistance put into an automobile ignition circuit to cut down excessive voltage.

Blow-by   Fuel or exhaust vapors that push past piston rings into the crankcase; caused by worn rings.

Bottom Dead Center   The lowest position a piston can be drawn in the cylinder; the opposite of Top Dead Center.

Breaker arm   The movable arm that the distributor cam lobe presses back to cause contact points to open.

Breaker points   Another name for contact points.

Cam (distributor)   The lobed rotor in the center of the distributor, which pushes open the contact points.

Cam angle   *See* Dwell angle.

166

Carburetor   A device for mixing air and fuel in the correct ratio to burn in the engine.

Centrifugal spark advance   Spring-loaded weights in the distributor. Distributor speed causes these weights to shift and advance the spark timing of the ignition.

Choke (v)   To close a valve in the distributor and cut off air in order to enrich the air/fuel ration.

Coil   An electrical device for increasing voltage.

Compression   The squeezing of the fuel in a cylinder into a smaller area in order to increase a car's power.

Compression ratio   The difference between the area of a piston at Bottom Dead Center and the size of the combustion chamber at Top Dead Center.

Condenser   An electrical "sponge" to absorb current when the breaker points open in the car's distributor. The condenser prevents arcing at the points.

Contact points   Two contacts through which the primary circuit of a car's ignition flows. Opening the points breaks the current.

Distributor   A device with a rotor inside to direct ignition current to the correct spark plug at the right time.

Dwell (dwell angle)   The time, expressed as degrees of a circle, during which the contact points in the distributor are closed. The amount of dwell determines build-up of high-tension current in the coil.

Dwell meter   A gauge for determining the correct dwell of a distributor.

Electrodes   The bottom terminals of a sparkplug.

Electrolyte   Mixture of water and sulfuric acid used in batteries.

Firing order   The numerical arrangement of the cylinders' firing.

Float   A floating device in the carburetor that regulates the flow of gas into the carburetor.

Generator   An electrical generating device putting out direct current; now replaced on new cars by an alternator which generates alternating current.

Ground   The connection of a car's electrical circuit to the body frame in order to complete the necessary complete circuit.

Heat range (of plugs)   The ability of a plug to transmit heat, resulting in "hot plugs" and "cold plugs."

High-tension wires   Refers to wires that carry the stepped-up voltage from coil to distributor and from distributor to individual spark-plugs.

Hydrometer   A device for checking the specific gravity of battery fluid.

Idle   The slow turning of an engine when the wheels are not moving.

Idle adjustment   Adjustment of the speed of the engine to obtain the correct idle speed.

Ignition system   A combination of battery, ignition switch, ballast resistor (on cars using it), coil, distributor, wiring and sparkplugs, all designed to cause ignition of the air/fuel mixture in the cylinders.

Induced current   Refers to the higher voltage "induced" in the secondary circuit of a coil by collapse of the magnetic field in the primary circuit.

In-line engine   An engine whose cylinders are arranged in a straight line.

Magnetic field   The flow of electricity through coiled wire wrapped around a soft iron core creates a "magnetic field" about the primary windings in the automobile coil.

Manifold, intake   A chamber attached to the engine block where fuel from the carburetor gathers until opening valves pull it into the cylinders.

Manifold, exhaust   A chamber attached to the engine block that receives the exhaust from the gases burned in the cylinder.

Ohm   A unit of measurement of resistance in a wire or circuit.

Ohmmeter   A device to measure electrical resistance.

Open circuit   A break in a wire or an open switch that prevents the flow of electricity.

Points, distributor   Contact points.

Positive Crankcase Ventilation (PCV)   A system to draw fumes from the crankcase to the intake manifold for reburning.

Primary circuit   The flow of battery current from the coil through the distributor points to ground.

PVC   *See* Positive Crankcase Ventilation.

Rotor   Something that rotates; generally in automobiles the rotating cap inside the distributor that makes contact with the inserts to direct current to the sparkplugs. In the Wankel engine "rotor" refers to the rotating device that replaces the piston in the standard automobile engine.

Secondary circuit The high-tension current induced by the collapse of the magnetic field in the coil. This is the current that fires the sparkplugs.

Short circuit Electricity follows the path of least resistance. If there is a shorter path it goes that way, bypassing the normal circuit.

Smog An irritating substance formed in the air by the action of sunlight on pollutants emitted by automobile exhausts.

Spark The leaping of electricity across the electrodes of a sparkplug—a flash of blue fire.

Spark advance An adjustment to cause the spark across the electrodes of a plug to occur earlier than originally set.

Sparkplug A device for creating a spark to fire the air/fuel mixture in the car's cylinders.

Spark retard An adjustment causing the spark to occur later.

Specific gravity The weight of a chemical in relation to water. Used to test the condition of a storage battery.

Sulfation The deteriorated condition of a battery.

Tach/dwell meter A gauge for measuring both the rpm and dwell of an engine.

Tachometer A device for measuring the rpm of an engine.

Timing Adjusting the spark to fire at the correct number of degrees before top dead center.

Timing light A stroboscopic light that makes timing marks on an engine appear to stand still so they can be adjusted.

Timing marks Engraved marks on a flywheel or fan-belt pulley or vibration dampener that permits a mechanic to determine the number of degrees the spark is firing before or after Top Dead Center.

Top Dead Center The highest position to which a piston can rise in the cylinder of a four-cycle engine.

Transistor ignition A distributor that does not have points but depends upon transistors to interrupt the primary current.

Tune-up Adjusting the ignition and carburetion of a car to factory specifications.

Vacuum In an automobile, lowered air pressure; not the true vacuum of physics, which means total absence of air.

Vacuum spark advance   A device attached to the carburetor for advancing the spark by suction of manifold vacuum against a diaphragm.

Venturi   A narrowed section of the air pipe in a carburetor.

Voltage   The pressure of an electrical current.

V-8 engine   An engine with two banks of cylinders opposing each other and joined by connecting rods to a joint crankshaft.

Wankel engine   The rotary engine used in the Mazda automobile.

Appendix

HOW TO REMOVE AND REPLACE
A DISTRIBUTOR

Removing the Distributor

1. Remove the distributor cap, leaving the wires attached. Disconnect the vacuum advance hose and remove the primary wire at the coil terminal.

2. Now mark the distributor and rotor position so you can get them back exactly as you removed them. It is best to tap the starter to get the rotor in the Number 1 plug firing position. Then note the direction in which the vacuum advance mechanism is pointing so you can get the distributor housing in correctly. Next mark the side of the distributor housing to indicate the position the rotor is pointing in relation to the housing. If it isn't pointing the same way upon reassembly, your engine will be out of time. If slightly out of time, it will start and you can retime with a timing light. If it's badly out of time, you may not even get it to run at all. Marking the position of distributor housing and rotor is thus very important.

3. Next loosen the hold-down bolt under the distributor as you were instructed in the chapter on timing an engine. Loosen it enough to permit you to slip the hold-down bracket out of the way of the hold-down flange on the

171

The rotor in the distributor should point to the Number 1 firing position before you remove the distributor. Mark this position on the side of the distributor body shell, for the distributor shaft will turn as it is removed. Marking the distributor makes it easy to replace.

distributor shaft. It is not usually necessary to remove the bracket entirely. Just loosen the hold-down bolt enough to push the bracket aside.

4. The distributor is then removed by lifting up. You will note that as the distributor is first lifted, it will turn slightly. The direction it turns depends upon whether the distributor normally rotates clockwise or counterclockwise. This slight turn is of no consequence in removing the distributor, but it will be very important in putting the distributor back in again. The reason the distributor turns slightly when you pull it up is because the drive gear on the

This shows a distributor removed from the car. Arrow points to the helical gear which meshes with a similar gear on the valve cam.

engine camshaft meshes with the gear on the distributor shaft. Both are helical gears. As you can see in the accompanying photograph of a pulled distributor, the gear teeth are set at an angle (indicated by arrow in the picture). These teeth mesh with similarly angled teeth in the cam. So when you pull up, the shaft cannot come straight out. It must turn slightly to allow the distributor gear to slide along the angled surface of the camshaft gear. The important thing is to note how much the distributor rotor turns away from the Number 1 plug position we previously marked. So when you put the shaft back in the engine, you begin by lining up these new marks, for the shaft will burn back just as much as it turned forward.

5. Once the distributor is removed, you can replace the points and condenser and check the movement of the centrifugal advance much more easily than on distributors that have not been removed.

Replacing the Distributor in the Car

1. Insert the distributor shaft into the hole in the block. Stop just before the gears mesh and line up the distributor body with the previous marks. At the same time move the rotor so that it points to the second mark made to show where the rotor turned to when lifted from the car on removal.

2. When the marks are aligned, push down on the distributor to mesh the distributor gear with the cam gear that drives it. If your alignment was correct, the rotor should move about 1/16th inch and line up with the mark you made to show the first position of the rotor on the number one firing position before you pulled the distributor.

3. If the marks do not align, you may be one tooth off on your gear mesh. Pull up the distributor until the gears separate, move the distributor one tooth either right or

left as necessary, and remesh the gears to bring the marks in line.

4. Replace the hold-down bracket over the shaft flange and tighten the hold-down bolt, but leave it sufficiently loose so that you can turn the distributor to time it.

5. Do not replace the distributor cap yet, but hold it over the distributor body, aligning it with the clips so that you are holding it exactly as it would fit. Note if the rotor does point toward the Number 1 plug insert in the cap. If you made your alignment marks correctly, it should. If it does not, follow directions given below.

6. If the rotor does point to or nearly to the Number 1 plug insert, put the cap aside temporarily. Replace the primary wire to the coil and plug the vacuum advance hose. Do not replace the vacuum advance hose on the distributor.

7. Hook up a test light. If it is the type with no battery, connect it to the distributor primary terminal and to ground. The light will be *off* when the points are closed. Turn the distributor in the opposite direction to its direction of rotation until the light comes on. If you have a powered timing light, you work a little differently. Take the primary wire off the coil and hook the test light to it and to ground as the light instructions will indicate. Then when you turn the distributor, the light will be *on* when the points are closed and will go off when they open. In either case, you are trying to determine as nearly as possible the exact instant the points begin to open.

8. Now check to see that the rotor is pointing to the Number 1 insert in the cap. If the points are just opening and the rotor points to the Number 1 firing position, then you are close enough in time to start the engine. Replace the distributor cap and the primary wire to the coil, if you removed it to use a powered test light.

9. Hook up your timing light, pointing it at the timing scale on the pulley or vibration dampener as instructed in the section on timing the engine. Leave the hold-down bolt loose so you can turn the distributor and check the engine timing to insure that it is according to specifications. After timing, replace vacuum advance hose.

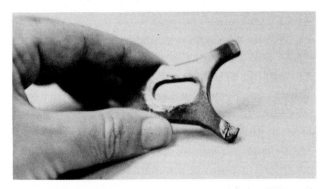

This is a typical hold-down bracket. The two arms fit around the flange on the distributor shaft and the elongated bolt hole permits the bracket to be shoved back when the hold-down bolt is loosened.

Replacing an Unmarked Distributor

In the above sequence you marked the positions of your distributor housing and rotor so that you could get them back correctly in the right relationship to each other. But what happens if you forget to mark the distributor, mark it wrong, or accidentally turn over the engine so that any marks you made cannot be used? In either case, you must reestablish an initial timing position. Here's how you do it.

1. Our objective is to get the distributor back in the engine so that the rotor is on the Number 1 plug insert when the engine is at *Top Dead Center* on the *compression stroke.* We must first find the compression stroke.
2. Remove the Number 1 sparkplug. Hook up a remote

starter switch. Then, as shown in the accompanying photograph, place your hand over the sparkplug hole. (Over it. Don't stick your fingers in the hole. And don't do this unless the engine is cold or you'll fry your hand on the hot manifold.)

3. Now with your fingers over the hole, turn over the engine with the remote starter. The engine will turn but won't start because you still have the cap off the distributor. When the piston comes up on the compression stroke you can feel the pressure on your fingers.

4. As soon as you feel this pressure and know you are coming up on the compression stroke, you can remove your fingers and watch the timing marks on the dampener or pulley. Keep tapping the switch to move the engine in small degrees until you line up the timing marks according to specs at the right number of degrees before top dead center.

5. The pressure on your fingers is quite noticeable, but if you have difficulty determining the compression stroke this way, then use a compression gauge in the Number 1 cylinder hole. You'll get no reading on the exhaust and intake strokes, but will see the gauge rise on the compression stroke. Once you see it begin to rise, forget the gauge. You don't need it any more. You used it only to help you determine which was the compression stroke.

6. Now shift your attention to the timing marks on the dampener and pulley. Keep tapping the remote starter switch to line up the timing marks according to timing specs just as you did in setting your initial timing. This means getting the timing mark opposite the correct degree scale.

7. Now line up the distributor rotor with the Number 1 plug insert in the distributor cap. Ease the assembly into the mounting hole in the block.

Here the mechanic is holding his fingers over the Number 1 spark plug hole to feel the pressure of the compression stroke.

8. Now check to see that the slight turning of the gears as they mesh did not move the rotor away from the Number 1 plug insert. Naturally you can't put the cap on or you can't see inside to determine the lineup, but hold it over the distributor and observe if the tower for the Number 1 cylinder plug wire seems to line up with the tip of the rotor. If so, partially tighten the hold-down bracket.

9. Now get your timing light hooked up and check out your timing. You shouldn't have to do much adjusting. Replace the distributor cap.

There is one little thing that may come up on some distributors. You may push the distributor into the mounting hole, feel the gears engage, and then find that the distributor shaft won't go all the way down. You can hammer on it until you break it but it won't go down.

Your trouble here is no trouble at all. It is just that this type of distributor has a tang in the end of the shaft—a recessed crosspiece of metal, designed to fit into a slot in the oil pump in order to drive the pump. It is just crosswise of the slot, which prevents the distributor shaft from going all the way down.

All you have to do is to press down on the distributor while you bip the starter button to turn the engine over. As soon as the tang in the distributor shaft lines up with the slot in the oil pump, the pressure you're putting on the distributor will seat the two.

No Problem

When the distributor is out of the car and you touch the starter button or otherwise cause the crankshaft to move, you mess up the timing and must reestablish TDC on the compression stroke. However, that does not happen here, because by the time the tang touches the oil pump the distributor gear and the camshaft gear are already half engaged and the two will turn together, maintaining their aligned position, when you hit the starter to move the distributor shaft so that the oil pump is engaged and the distributor shaft will seat.

INDEX

182 ◯ **Index**

184 ◯ **Index**